CAMBRIDGE
NORFOLK & SUFFOLK
UNLOCKED

by
Chloe Jeffries

il

edited by
Emily Kerr & Joshua Perry

CAMBRIDGE

CAMBRIDGESHIRE

SUFFOLK

NORWICH

NORFOLK

TOP FIVES

This book belongs to:

CAMBRIDGE
CAMBRIDGESHIRE
SUFFOLK
NORWICH
NORFOLK
TOP FIVES

CONTENTS

CAMBRIDGE

CAMBRIDGESHIRE

SUFFOLK

NORWICH

NORFOLK

TOP FIVES

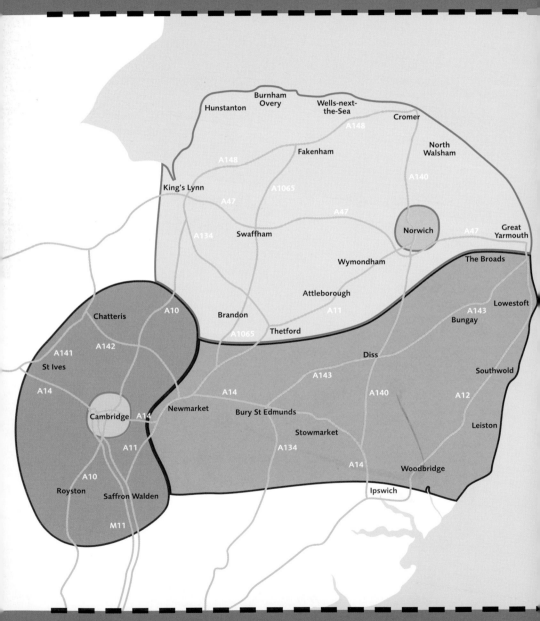

SUFFOLK

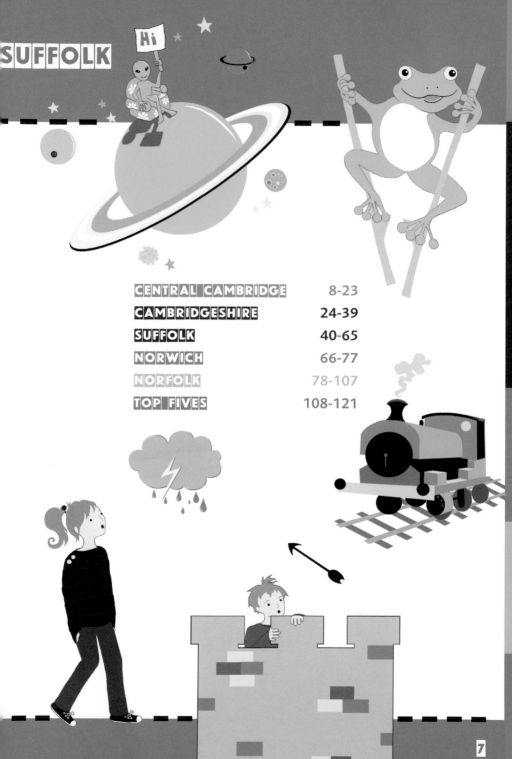

CAMBRIDGE

CAMBRIDGESHIRE

SUFFOLK

NORWICH

NORFOLK

TOP FIVES

CENTRAL CAMBRIDGE

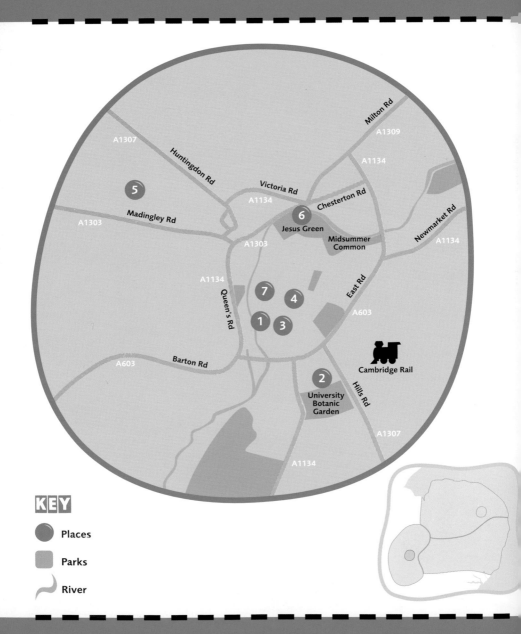

A1307
Milton Rd
A1309
Huntingdon Rd
A1134
Victoria Rd
Chesterton Rd
5
A1134
6
Newmarket Rd
Madingley Rd
Jesus Green
A1303
Midsummer Common
A1134
A1303
East Rd
A1134
Queen's Rd
7
4
A603
1 **3**
Cambridge Rail
Barton Rd
A603
2
University Botanic Garden
Hills Rd
A1307
A1134

KEY

● Places

■ Parks

〜 River

CAMBRIDGE

CAMBRIDGESHIRE

SUFFOLK

NORWICH

NORFOLK

TOP FIVES

TAKE A WATER TAXI

...along the river Cam

Taxis don't usually go along rivers. And taxi drivers don't usually wear straw hats. But both are traditional in Cambridge where you can be driven through the city on a punt!

A punt is a large flat-bottomed boat propelled by a pole. You can hire chauffeured or unchauffeured punts from several companies by the river Cam (Scudamore's is particularly popular).

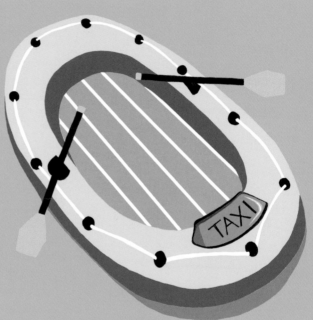

Sticker Scores

5	**4**	**3**
POLE STAR	*OAR*-SOME	WORTH A PUNT
2	**1**	
FLAT BOTTOMED	STUCK IN THE MUD	

Punting is a great way to see the old university buildings and bridges. It's also much more difficult than it sounds – if you take an unchauffeured punt you'll need a strong grown-up with you. Just make sure they don't fall in . . .

Make A Day Of It

🔑 Glide to Grantchester.
Grantchester meadows are three miles along the Cam and are the perfect place for picnics. Legend has it that a secret underground tunnel runs from Grantchester back to Cambridge (but we haven't found it yet).

Photo Op

Get a snap of you lounging back in your boat. Make sure the person punting is in the shot too!

← Mind your head!

Fascinating Facts

⭐ **Clare College bridge (which your punt will pass under) is decorated with fourteen stone balls. One has a missing wedge that looks like a piece cut out of a round cheese. Some people say this is because the bridge builder was not paid the full amount for his work and so removed a section in anger!**

⭐ The fancy covered bridge by St John's College (known as the Bridge of Sighs) has been the site of some spectacular pranks. On two occasions cheeky students have dangled a car underneath it! We think that's *car*-azy!

⭐ **Cambridge has a muddy riverbed, so the punting pole sometimes gets stuck. If that happens to you then let go – it's better to lose the pole than end up in the water!**

PLAN YOUR VISIT ①

Scudamore's Punting Company
Granta Place, Mill Lane, Cambridge, CB2 1RS
www.scudamores.com

📞 **01223 359750**

🕐 **Daily (summer) 09.00-21.00**
Daily (out of season) 10.00-17.30

£££

I want to go here ☐

MEET A MEAT-EATING PLANT

...at the Botanic Garden

Most plants get all the food they need from the soil and the air. However, there are a few that actually eat other animals. Fortunately they don't grow big enough to chomp on humans – they devour insects instead!

The Cambridge University Botanic Garden has a large collection of carnivorous plants in its glasshouses. Each plant has developed a different way of landing its lunch. Sticky sundews get their prey by capturing them in the little globules of glue they have in their tentacles, and Venus flytraps snap shut suddenly on their victims.

Our favourite is the pesky pitcher plant, which lures insects before drowning them in a pool of poison. They look innocent, but for unfortunate flies they are a venomy enemy!

Sticker Scores

5 ALL THE TRAPPINGS

4 FLY FEAST

3 MEATY MEAL

2 INSECT INDIGESTION

1 YOU'RE LUNCH

What do you call a man with a cactus on his head?

Spike!

Don't put your finger in the meat-eating plants!

Best Of The Rest

🔑 Pass some prickly plants in the Cactus House.

🔑 Buzz along to the Bee Border. It's full of flowers of every colour except red, which bees can't see.

Top Tip

Borrow a Young Explorer backpack from the ticket office. The kit contains binoculars, a magnifying glass and a clipboard!

Fascinating Facts

★ Plants have an amazing ability to extract food from thin air! The process is called photosynthesis and involves using the energy in sunlight to convert air into sugar and other things. We wish we could pluck a plate of chips out of the sky!

★ When the Venus flytrap is hungry, its leaves open wide. On the leaves are short, sensitive hairs called 'trigger hairs'. When anything touches these hairs enough to bend them, the two halves of the leaf will snap shut, trapping whatever is inside in less than a second.

★ The saguaro is a cactus which can grow up to seventeen metres high. That's taller than a five-storey building (but harder to live in)!

PLAN YOUR VISIT ②

Cambridge University Botanic Garden

1 Brookside, Cambridge, CB2 1JE

www.botanic.cam.ac.uk

📞 01223 336265

🕐 Daily (summer) 10.00-18.00
Daily (out of season) 10.00-16.00

I want to go here ☐

SCRAMBLE OVER SCULPTURE

...at the Fitzwilliam Museum

Normally we wouldn't suggest that you spend a day staring at sculptures. But the Fitzwilliam Museum has found a way to make it fun – by turning its front lawn into an arty playground!

The Fitzwilliam is Cambridge's biggest art museum. Each summer they transform part of the grounds into a Sculpture Promenade – and they even let you touch the objects. The sculptures are crafted for the museum by modern artists, so you won't find any carvings by boring dead people!

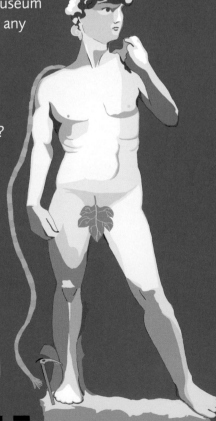

Some of the sculptures are squishy and some feel like skin. One is wind powered and another dances. Why not draw a picture of your favourite? The museum will give you paper and pencils. Go on, you'd be *art*less to miss it!

Sticker Scores

5 — SUPER SCULPTURE

4 — AMAZING ART

3 — COOL CARVING

2 — SATISFACTORY STATUE

1 — SCRAP METAL

Best Of The Rest

 The ancient Egyptian gallery in the museum contains some marvellous mummy cases. Look out for the *Book of the Dead*, which contains spells to help a person pass into the afterlife!

← Sitting inside a sculpture

Top Tip
The museum runs art workshops on Saturdays. You'll need to book ahead.

Fascinating Facts

★ **Alaska, in the United States, hosts the World Ice Sculpting Championships each year. Teams must create a subzero masterpiece from a four-tonne block of ice. They have two days to complete their sculpture and no machinery is allowed.**

★ The record for the world's largest cheese sculpture is held by British chef Tanys Pullen. She spent 100 hours carving a 500-kilogramme replica of the Queen's coronation crown out of cheddar!

★ **At Mount Rushmore, also in the US, the heads of four former presidents have been sculpted into the side of the mountain. The carvings are so huge that they can be seen from 60 miles away!**

PLAN YOUR VISIT ③

The Fitzwilliam Museum
Trumpington Street, Cambridge, CB2 1RB
www.fitzmuseum.cam.ac.uk

📞 **01223 332900**

🕐 **Tue-Sat 10.00-17.00**
   Sun & Bank Hol 12.00-17.00

FREE 🎁

I want to go here ☐

SCREAM AT THE WORLD'S LARGEST SPIDER

...at the Sedgwick Museum of Earth Sciences

It would be difficult to flush the world's largest spider down the plughole as its legs are over 50 centimetres long! Fortunately it's unlikely to sneak up on you because it's also been dead for millions of years . . .

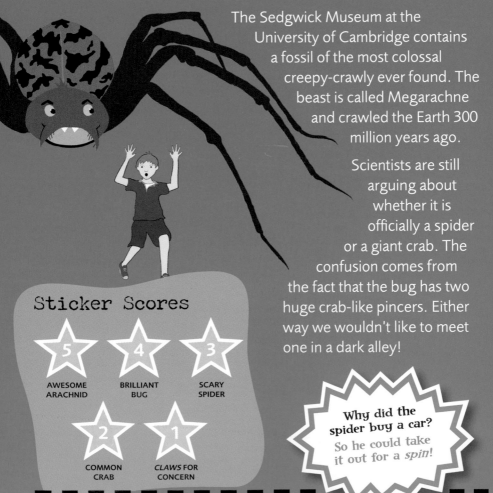

The Sedgwick Museum at the University of Cambridge contains a fossil of the most colossal creepy-crawly ever found. The beast is called Megarachne and crawled the Earth 300 million years ago.

Scientists are still arguing about whether it is officially a spider or a giant crab. The confusion comes from the fact that the bug has two huge crab-like pincers. Either way we wouldn't like to meet one in a dark alley!

Sticker Scores

5 — AWESOME ARACHNID

4 — BRILLIANT BUG

3 — SCARY SPIDER

2 — COMMON CRAB

1 — *CLAWS* FOR CONCERN

Why did the spider buy a car?
So he could take it out for a *spin*!

Best Of The Rest

 Delve into the Darwin Discovery Chest – a treasure trove of puzzles relating to the famous scientist Charles Darwin.

 Touch terrifying teeth. The museum's handling collection includes gnashers from a dinosaur, a shark and even a sabre-toothed tiger!

← "Aaaaarrrrgggghhhh!"

Top Tip
The museum will identify any rock, mineral or fossil specimen on the spot for free. Take along any find from your back garden. You never know – you might have hit upon buried treasure!

Fascinating Facts

★ Spiders are not insects but in fact belong to a group of animals called arachnids. Arachnids have two body segments, eight legs, no wings or antennae and are not able to chew. Insects have six legs and three main body parts. See if you can catch a grown-up out with this fact!

★ Spiders have 48 knees! That's because they have eight legs with six joints on each. Why not find yourself a spider and count its knees?

★ A spider's body is covered in a special oil to stop it from sticking to its own web.

PLAN YOUR VISIT ④

The Sedgwick Museum of Earth Sciences
Downing Street, Cambridge, CB2 3EQ
www.sedgwickmuseum.org

📞 01223 333456

🕐 Mon-Fri 10.00-13.00 and 14.00-17.00
Sat 10.00-16.00

FREE

I want to go here ☐

STARGAZE WITH ASTRONOMERS

...at the Institute of Astronomy

On a clear night you can see the Moon and bright stars with the naked eye. So just think how much of the galaxy you could see if you were looking through the lens of a giant telescope!

The Institute of Astronomy run space-observation evenings once a week. The session begins with a short talk, followed by a look through huge historical telescopes.

You can also stargaze (or gaze) through three very powerful modern telescopes set up outside. Each is equipped with an electronic camera which projects images from the telescope onto huge screens.

Visitors have spotted shooting stars, Saturn, Venus and Mars. Sadly no one's spotted an alien . . . yet!

Sticker Scores

⭐ 5 SUPER STAR	⭐ 4 BRIGHT STAR	⭐ 3 LUCKY STAR
⭐ 2 FADING STAR	⭐ 1 *STAR*-VING	

Fascinating Facts

★ The huge Hubble Space Telescope can see faraway objects more clearly than any telescope in history. Unfortunately it's quite tricky to pay a visit to the telescope as it's currently orbiting Earth (you'll have to wait for *Outer Space Unlocked*)!

★ The hottest planet in our solar system is Venus. It has a surface temperature of about 450 degrees Celsius. That's twice as hot as the maximum temperature on a normal oven!

★ Footprints and tyre tracks left behind by astronauts on the Moon will stay there for ever as there is no wind to blow them away.

⌐ Let us know if you spot an alien

What do you call an unhappy spaceship?
A crying saucer!

Top Tip
Wrap up warm when you visit as it can get quite chilly at night! If it's particularly cold you'll also be given a hot drink to keep your spirits up.

PLAN YOUR VISIT 5

Institute of Astronomy
Madingley Road, Cambridge, CB3 OHA
www.ast.cam.ac.uk

📞 01223 337548

🕐 Wed (Oct-Mar) 19.00-21.00

FREE

I want to go here ☐

SWIM IN BRITAIN'S LONGEST OUTDOOR POOL

...at Jesus Green Lido

Y ou can't go swimming in Cambridge's river – it's far too slimy. But you can make a splash in the next best thing – an outdoor swimming pool designed to look like a river!

A lido is a type of open-air pool, and Jesus Green has one of the longest lidos in Europe. At 91 metres it's almost four times longer than a standard swimming pool.

It runs alongside the river Cam and is long and thin so that it feels like you're swimming in a river. The water in the pool is also taken from the river – but don't worry, it's cleaned carefully to remove the creepy-crawlies first!

Sticker Scores

⭐ **5** — CRACKING CRAWL

⭐ **4** — BRILLIANT BREASTSTROKE

⭐ **3** — BASIC BACKSTROKE

⭐ **2** — DODGY DOGGY PADDLE

⭐ **1** — BELLY FLOP

Similar Spots

🔑 If you prefer to paddle, head to the smaller Lammas Land Outdoor Pool near the Fen Causeway in Cambridge. It's also next to a good playground.

🔑 When the weather's bad, head to the indoor Parkside Pool in the city centre. It has a leisure pool and two flume rides.

What gets wetter as it dries?
A towel!

← See if you can swim a length!

Fascinating Facts

⭐ The first man to swim the English Channel (the stretch of water between Britain and France) was Captain Matthew Webb, in 1875. It took him just under 22 hours and he smeared himself in porpoise oil to keep warm. Sadly Captain Webb's love of lunatic swimming challenges proved to be fatal – he died eight years later while attempting to swim the rapids of Niagara Falls.

⭐ Elephants can swim for up to twenty miles underwater, using their trunks as snorkels! We wonder where they buy their goggles . . .

PLAN YOUR VISIT ⑥

Jesus Green Outdoor Pool
off Chesterton Road, Cambridge, CB5 8AL
www.cambridge.gov.uk

📞 01223 302579

🕐 Mon, Wed, Thu (summer) 12.00-19.30
Tue, Fri (summer) 07.30-19.30
Sat-Sun (summer) 11.00-19.30

£

I want to go here ☐

CHANT IN THE CHAPEL OF A MURDERED KING

...at King's College

We all make excuses for not finishing things like homework or tidying up, but the man who started building King's College has a pretty good reason for not finishing the chapel – he was locked up in prison and then killed!

Construction of King's College's chapel was begun by King Henry VI in 1446. However, nine years after the first stone was laid, war broke out with a rival family over who should rule. Henry was imprisoned and killed in the Tower of London, so it was left to later kings to complete the magnificent structure.

Today, King's College chapel is home to a famous choir, which includes sixteen schoolboys from nearby King's College School. You can sing along with them at one of the term-time evensong services. It's an en-*chant*-ing experience!

Sticker Scores

5 PERFECT HARMONY

4 CRACKING CAROL

3 HEAVENLY HYMN

2 STANDARD SONG

1 OUT OF TUNE

Best Of The Rest

 Cambridge is full of colleges – 31 in total. They are part of the city's famous university and many are open to the public, so you can walk around them and see how the students live. We particularly like these two:

Trinity College holds a running race each year called the Great Court Run. The aim is to run around the college's Great Court within the time that it takes for the college clock to chime twelve.

Magdalene College is built on one side of a bend in the river. This was a deliberate design feature to separate the monks who used to study at this college from the temptations of the town on the other side!

← Check out the chapel

Fascinating Facts

★ Henry VI was just nine months old when he became king. A group of advisors helped him govern until he was sixteen to make sure he didn't spend the royal budget on toys and sweets!

★ Henry came up with the rule that the chapel choir had to contain sixteen poor boys under the age of twelve who could read and sing. Sixteen choristers (choir boys) are still recruited each year. It's not compulsory to be poor any more though!

★ At Christmas the chapel holds a carol service which is broadcast on TV around the world. The first carol is always 'Once in Royal David's City'. The chorister who will be singing the solo in this carol is not told until immediately before the service begins!

Top Tip

Combine a visit to the chapel with a stop at the **Fudge Kitchen** on King's Parade. They sell the finest fudge in the city!

PLAN YOUR VISIT 7

King's College Chapel

King's Parade, Cambridge, CB2 1ST

www.kings.cam.ac.uk

☎ 01223 331315

🕐 Mon-Sat (peak) 09.30-16.30,
Sun 10.00-17.00
Mon-Fri (out of season) 09.30 – 15.30
Sat 09.30-15.15, Sun 13.15-14.15
Evensong: Mon-Wed & Fri-Sat
(term-time) 17.30

FREE ☂

I want to go here ☐

CAMBRIDGESHIRE

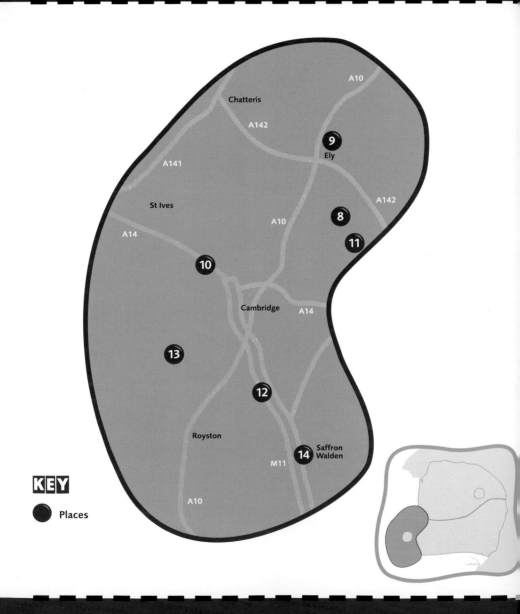

Chatteris

A10

A142

9
Ely

A141

St Ives

A142

A10

8

A14

A10

11

10

Cambridge

A14

13

12

Royston

Saffron
Walden

14

M11

A10

KEY

Places

CAMBRIDGE

CAMBRIDGESHIRE

SUFFOLK

NORWICH

NORFOLK

TOP FIVES

WATCH DRAGONFLIES

...at Wicken Fen

Stilts are not just for circus performers. Traditionally the only way of crossing the fen marshes was by walking on two long poles! Fortunately these are no longer needed – you can explore the area's amazing wildlife by walking along the boardwalks . . .

A fen is an area of low-lying wetland. Much of East Anglia was fen land until it was drained in the seventeenth century to make it more suitable for farming. Wicken is one of the few undrained fens.

This rare habitat makes Wicken a happy home for butterflies, frogs and otters. It's also one of the best places in the country to watch dragonflies. On warm days you can catch up to 21 brightly coloured species performing aerial acrobatics above the waterways!

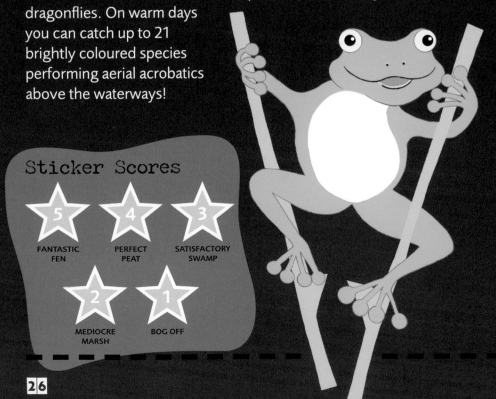

Sticker Scores

5 FANTASTIC FEN

4 PERFECT PEAT

3 SATISFACTORY SWAMP

2 MEDIOCRE MARSH

1 BOG OFF

Best Of The Rest

🔑 Go pond-dipping for mini monsters in the streams. Nets are provided.

🔑 Walk with wild ponies. Konik ponies have recently been reintroduced at Wicken Fen. They are the nearest living ancestors to the type of wild horses that once roamed Europe.

🔑 Listen out for cuckoos at the start of spring. They lay their eggs in the nests of other birds, and then leave them to look after their babies.

What do you call an Irish Dragonfly?
Paddy-Longlegs!

← Pond-dipping at Wicken Fen

Fascinating Facts

★ Wicken Fen is one of Britain's oldest nature reserves, and the first reserve purchased by the National Trust. They bought it in 1899 for just £10 – that's about the same price as this book!

★ The draining of the fens dramatically changed the shape of the coastline. The towns of Wisbech and Spalding were once ports but now they are several miles inland!

★ There was fierce opposition to the draining of the fens. Local people felt the scheme threatened their traditional way of life, which was based on fishing, and so launched a campaign to keep the area marshy. They destroyed drainage machinery and were nicknamed the Fen Tigers.

PLAN YOUR VISIT ⑧

Wicken Fen National Nature Reserve
Lode Lane, Wicken, Ely, CB7 5XP
www.wicken.org.uk

📞 01353 720274

🕐 Daily (summer) 10.00-17.00
Daily (out of season) 10.00-16.30

I want to go here ☐

MAKE YOUR OWN STAINED-GLASS WINDOW

...at Ely Cathedral

Usually windows are just something you look through. But in the Middle Ages, before most people could read, they were used to tell stories.

Stained-glass windows contain lots of bits of coloured glass held together by a web of lead. The coloured pieces form a picture from a well-known story. Then when the sun shines through, the whole image lights up.

High up inside Ely Cathedral you can make your own stained-glass panel in the Stained Glass Museum. You choose your design and use the special glass paint provided. Luckily the cathedral already has over 100 stained-glass windows so you're allowed to take yours home!

Sticker Scores

5 SMASHING STAINED GLASS

4 WONDERFUL WINDOW

3 COOL COLOURS

2 PLAIN PORTHOLE

1 *PANE* IN THE NECK

Photo Op
Sit on top of the old canon on the green with the cathedral tower behind you. Make the person taking the photo shout, 'Ready, Aim, FIRE!'.

Make A Day Of It

🔑 Call into Oliver Cromwell's house. Cromwell took charge of England in the 1600s after helping to execute King Charles I. While in power he banned brightly coloured dresses, football and Christmas. Thankfully his house is much more fun!

🔑 Follow the Ely Eel Trail. The trail is marked by pictures of eels set into the ground. It starts at Cromwell's house and leads through Cherry Hill Park to the river Ouse.

🔑 Sample a smoked eel at Ely Farmers' market on Saturdays. Eels from the river Ouse are usually on sale. D-*eel*-icious!

← An Ely impressive cathedral!

Fascinating Facts

⭐ Stained-glass-window painters use brushes made from badger hair. Presumably you need several brushes to have a full *sett*!

⭐ In the sixteenth century, hundreds of monasteries (homes for monks) were closed down in England as part of a huge argument between King Henry VIII and the Pope. Their stained-glass windows were smashed and replaced with plain glass.

⭐ Glass paint contains a mixture of copper filings, gum and a liquid such as wine, vinegar or, in the past, urine! Luckily *wee* don't paint like this any more . . .

PLAN YOUR VISIT ⑨

The Stained Glass Museum
The South Triforium, Ely Cathedral, Ely, CB7 4DL
www.stainedglassmuseum.com

🎧 01353 660347

🕐 Mon-Fri 10.30-17.00, Sat 10.30-17.30
Sun 12.00-18.00

I want to go here ☐

BECOME AN UNDERCOVER AGENT

...at Spymasters

A full-time job as a spy would be exciting, but you'd probably have to change your name and your appearance. However, at Spymasters you can experience the thrill of being an undercover agent without losing your identity!

Spymasters is an indoor activity centre which lets you take on the role of a spy. Upon arrival you will be given details of your 'mission'. You then start a challenge against the clock that requires quick thinking and agility.

Your team will have to crack codes, solve puzzles, dodge motion detectors and use numerous spy gadgets, before a final adrenalin-fuelled escape. Now that's what we call a game of I-spy!

Sticker Scores

5 SUPER SLEUTH

4 EXCELLENT ESPIONAGE

3 CRACKING CODE

2 DASTARDLY DISGUISE

1 MISSION IMPOSSIBLE

← OPEN

04:23:60

Fascinating Facts

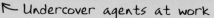

⭐ Cambridge has a history of spying. The Cambridge Five were a group of students at Cambridge University who were recruited as spies by the Russian government. They passed official British secrets to the Russians during the 1940s and 1950s, but they weren't uncovered for many years and one of the spies even became art advisor to the Queen!

⭐ The most famous fictional spy is James Bond. Bond is famous for driving cool cars, including amazing Aston Martins, a Russian tank (*GoldenEye*), a double-decker bus (*Live and Let Die*) and an oil tanker (*Licence to Kill*).

⌐ Undercover agents at work

What do secret agents eat at Christmas? Mince *spies!*

Photo Op
Strike your best super-sleuth pose upon completing your mission.

PLAN YOUR VISIT ⑩

Spymasters
7 Viking Way, Bar Hill, Cambridge, CB23 8EL
www.spymasters.co.uk

📞 01954 789134

🕐 Tue-Sun 10.00-19.00

£££

I want to go here ☐

WALK THE DEVIL'S DYKE

...at Reach

The countryside around Cambridge is very flat. So whenever you see a mound or hill, there is often a mysterious story behind it.

Devil's Dyke is a high bank of earth which runs between the villages of Reach and Burwell. It was probably built by the Anglo-Saxons to defend against invaders. However, local legend offers another explanation . . . The story goes that the devil came uninvited to a wedding at Reach church and was chased away by guests. He stormed off in anger and formed the groove of Devil's Dyke with his fiery tail.

The walk along the top of the bank features fantastic views, rare butterflies and blackberries to pick in autumn. Just don't eat all the fruit before you *Reach* your destination!

Sticker Scores

5 DEVILISH DYKE

4 VICIOUS VALLEY

3 SATANIC SLOPE

2 HUMBLE HILL

1 BANK-RUPT

Photo Op

The fens surrounding Reach are famous for their spectacular sunsets. If you're walking the dyke as the sun is setting, get someone to take a photo of you on the bank with the sun behind you. Hold up your hands to make it look like you're pinching the sun!

How did the devil teach his pupils? With lots of *demon*-strations!

Top Tip

The Reach Fair is held on the early May bank holiday every year. There are swing boats, a cake walk and even maypole dancing.

← Devil's Dyke

Fascinating Facts

⭐ Another local legend is the tale of Black Shuck. Black Shuck is the name given to a large demonic dog that reportedly roams the East Anglian countryside. The huge hound is said to have big burning eyes. Anyone unfortunate enough to look into them will supposedly die within twelve months.

⭐ In 1727 Burwell suffered a terrible tragedy. A barn where a puppet show was being performed was set on fire when a person carrying a candle peeped through the window. 78 people died, including 51 children. Look out for the gravestone commemorating the dead in St Mary's churchyard. It is engraved with a heart on fire, angels' wings and a skull.

PLAN YOUR VISIT 11

Devil's Dyke

The Dyke's End Pub, 8 Fair Green, Reach, CB25 0JD (Start walk from here)

www.dykesend.co.uk

 01638 743816

FREE

I want to go here ☐

COME NOSE TO NOSE WITH A SPITFIRE

...at Imperial War Museum Duxford

Despite its name, a Spitfire plane doesn't throw flames! In fact, these days the Spitfires at Duxford can't even fly . . . but they are great fun to visit!

The Imperial War Museum at Duxford holds over 30 military and civilian aircraft in its huge hall. You can get up close to these fabulous flying machines, and in the case of Concorde (a now-retired passenger plane that flew faster than the speed of sound) you can even climb aboard!

The World War Two fighter planes are amongst the most impressive exhibits. Look underneath the marvellous Mosquito, and then admire the speedy Spitfires. If you're a fan of awesome aircraft you certainly won't be com-*plane*-ing!

Sticker Scores

5 FEARSOME FIGHTER

4 JUMBO JET

3 PROPELLER PLANE

2 GRACEFUL GLIDER

1 *PLANE BORING*

Best Of The Rest

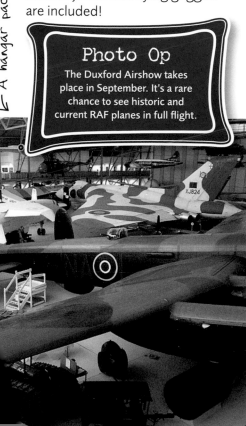

↖ A hangar packed with planes

🗝 Take cover inside a World War Two air-raid shelter.

🗝 Learn how to pilot a plane at the hands-on exhibits in the AirSpace zone.

🗝 Board a biplane. The Classic Wings tour at Duxford airfield offers trips over the surrounding countryside in one of these amazing double-winged contraptions. Leather jacket and flying goggles are included!

Photo Op
The Duxford Airshow takes place in September. It's a rare chance to see historic and current RAF planes in full flight.

Fascinating Facts

★ **The Spitfire was a British single-seat fighter plane that played an important role in World War Two. Some of the Spitfires were modified to carry small beer barrels under their wings instead of bombs. Troops on the continent were particularly happy when these planes arrived!**

★ The aircraft hall at Duxford was built around the machines. This means that many of the larger planes – like Concorde – can never come out without demolishing the building!

★ **The longest recorded paper-plane flight is 27.6 seconds. The plane was made with one sheet of paper, no scissors and no glue. It was thrown in a hangar at Tokyo airport (not across a classroom!).**

PLAN YOUR VISIT 12

Imperial War Museum Duxford
Duxford Airfield, Duxford, Cambridge, CB22 4QR
www.iwm.org.uk

📞 01223 835000

🕐 Daily (peak) 10.00-18.00
Daily (out of season) 10.00-16.00

££

I want to go here ☐

FEED RARE FARM ANIMALS

...at Wimpole Hall

Have you ever been told you eat like a pig? And have you ever wondered whether that's true?

At Wimpole Hall Home Farm you can find out exactly how pigs – and many other animals – really eat. It is a fully working farm, meaning that there are always lots of chores to do, like feeding pigs and milking cows. Many of the animals are rare breeds not usually seen on farms. Visitors are encouraged to muck in (and sometimes even go *in* muck!).

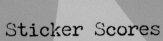

Sticker Scores

5	**4**	**3**
SWINE DINING	FARMYARD FEAST	BARNYARD BANQUET
2	**1**	
STABLE SNACK	GREEDY PIG	

A shire-horse wagon ride takes you over to the magnificent hall, which is the largest country house in Cambridgeshire. Its gardens also contain an adventure playground made from old tractors. You'll have a *swill* time!

Make A Day Of It

Descend deep underground at nearby Royston Caves. This mysterious man-made cavern is shaped like a bee hive and is decorated with historic carvings.

← Farm animals aren't allowed on the lawn!

> **What do you call a pig thief?**
> **A hamburglar!**

Top Tip

If you visit the farm during lambing season, you may get the chance to bottle-feed the babies. Most lambs arrive between March and April, so at this time of year farmers need to be on standby 24 hours a day.

Fascinating Facts

★ **Pigs cannot sweat because they have no sweat glands. Instead, they roll around in mud to cool their skin.**

★ Pigs are one of the only animals other than humans that can get sunburn. Presumably, if they spend too long in the sun they have to put on *oink*ment!

★ **Tamworth, Berkshire and Gloucester Old Spot are three of the rare pig breeds at Wimpole Hall Home Farm. Old Spots are also sometimes known as Orchard Pigs as they were traditionally kept in orchards where they would eat the fallen apples.**

★ The scream of a frightened pig can measure 115 decibels (a scale for measuring noise levels). The sound of a jumbo jet taking off measures around 113 decibels!

PLAN YOUR VISIT 13

Wimpole Hall Home Farm
Wimpole Estate, Royston, SG8 0BW
www.wimpole.org

📞 01223 206000

🕐 **Daily (summer) 10.30-17.00**
Sat-Sun (out of season) 11.00-16.00

I want to go here ☐

PLAY CROQUET

...at Audley End

You might not expect to find a sports pitch at a smart stately home. However, there is one game we like that is also loved by lords and ladies: croquet!

The flat lawns outside Audley End house are the perfect site for a spot of croquet. You'll be given all the equipment (mallets, wickets, balls) and a simple rule book. Divide into two teams and try to hit the ball between the hoop-like wickets.

The game might start off politely, but as things heat up you can play a number of ruthless moves, such as hitting your opponent's ball into the flowerbeds! The aim is to *hammer* the opposition (but not literally!).

Sticker Scores

5	4	3
CROQUET CHAMPION	LAWN LEGEND	MALLET MAN

2	1
BALL BASHER	*HOOP-LESS*

Best Of The Rest

🔑 Ride a steam train. The miniature Audley End Express takes you through the estate and woods.

🔑 Listen to music in the woods. Audley End's summer picnic concerts are hugely popular. Check out www.picnicconcerts.com for more information.

← Anyone for croquet?

Photo Op
Get a snap of you swinging your mallet and roaring like a ruthless croquet warrior!

What is a frog's favourite sport? *Croak*-et!

Fascinating Facts

⭐ **Croquet made it to the bottom of the world in 2005, when American scientists played a game outside the South Pole Observatory! We reckon that's pretty *cool*!**

⭐ Lewis Carroll featured a surreal version of croquet in *Alice in Wonderland*. A hedgehog was used as the ball, a flamingo became the mallet and soldiers doubled over to create the hoops. We recommend that you stick to the conventional version!

⭐ **Croquet has been reinvented in many forms. Extreme croquet features sand, mud and water hazards. Meanwhile, two million people partake in gateball, a Japanese form of five-a-side croquet played at speed!**

PLAN YOUR VISIT 14
Audley End House and Gardens
Saffron Walden, CB11 4JF
www.english-heritage.org.uk
📞 01799 522842
🕐 Wed-Sun (peak) 11.00-18.00

££

I want to go here ☐

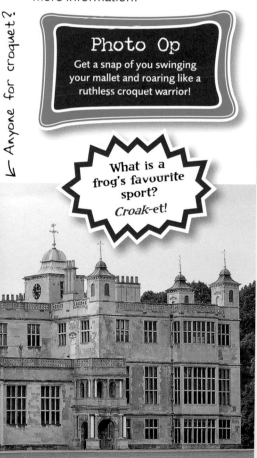

SUFFOLK

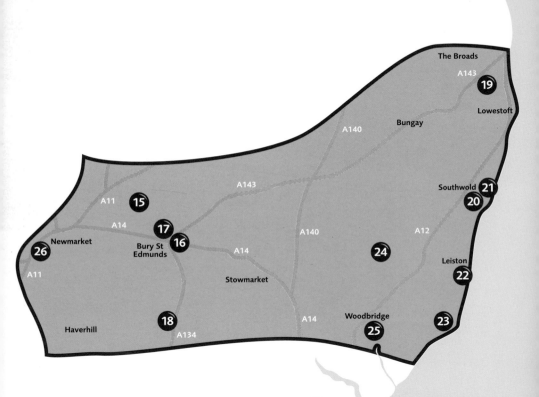

The Broads

A143

19

Lowestoft

A140

Bungay

A143

Southwold **21**

20

A11 **15**

A14

17

16

A140

A12

26 Newmarket

Bury St
Edmunds

24

A11

A14

Leiston

22

Stowmarket

Woodbridge

23

18

A14

25

Haverhill

A134

KEY

 Places

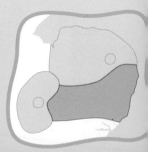

CAMBRIDGE

CAMBRIDGESHIRE

SUFFOLK

NORWICH

NORFOLK

TOP FIVES

EXPLORE A DARK-AGE VILLAGE

...at West Stow

The Dark Ages lasted for 600 years, but that doesn't mean that it was pitch black for six centuries! In fact it's the name used to refer to the Saxon period from 410 to 1066 AD.

West Stow is a reconstruction of an Anglo-Saxon village on its original site. Historians used to think that the Saxons were simple savages, but thanks to archaeological discoveries at sites like West Stow we now know that the Saxons got up to lots of smart stuff. They perfected pottery and jewellery making and were great story tellers.

You can even have a go at several Saxon crafts on certain days. Try making felt, designing a shield or brewing herbal potions. And don't worry, there's no need to bring a torch!

Sticker Scores

5 — MUD MANSION

4 — HANDSOME HUT

3 — CLASSY CABIN

2 — COLD CAVE

1 — SHODDY SHED

Photo Op

Find the banquet hut with the throne. Sit on it and look powerful for the camera!

Fascinating Facts

★ Historians called the Saxon period the Dark Ages because they knew very little about it compared to the Roman period that came before. So we're all in the *dark* as to what went on!

★ Saxon houses had no chimneys – the smoke just drifted upwards and out through a hole in the roof. When a pig was killed for food it was hung above the roof and the smoke cured it so that the meat wouldn't go off. So a pig killed in autumn could still be eaten in spring.

★ To build a house the Saxons planted posts in the ground then wove branches between them. The gaps were then plastered over with mud and pig droppings! Pig poo is particularly sticky, apparently . . .

★ Saxons wove clothes out of crushed, dried plants such as stinging nettles. Thankfully people no longer think it's a good idea to wear knickers made from nettles!

"Are you sure you're from the Dark Ages?"

PLAN YOUR VISIT 15

West Stow Country Park and Anglo-Saxon Village

Icklingham Road, West Stow, Bury St Edmunds, IP28 6HG

www.stedmundsbury.gov.uk

☎ 01284 728718

🕐 Daily (peak) 10.00-16.00
Daily (out of season) 10.00-15.30

I want to go here ☐

Top Tip

Archaeologists are still unearthing new finds around West Stow. The Bury Young Archaeologists Club organise regular digs and are always keen for volunteers to get muddy! Check the club's website for details.

SUFFOLK

GO BACKSTAGE

...at the Theatre Royal, Bury St Edmunds

When the red curtain goes down, the show may be over. But there's a lot more to theatres than what happens on the stage . . .

The Theatre Royal in Bury St Edmunds is the only Regency (early nineteenth century) theatre in the county open to the public. Look out for the tiny curved stage, high boxes and narrow rows of seats – they're all typical of the period.

Take a backstage tour to find out how the sound, lighting and actors' wardrobes work. You can also climb up close to the newly restored gold-leaf decoration and *trompe d'oeil* wall paintings (paintings that play tricks on the eye). For the full theatrical experience, stay and see one of the kids' shows.

Sticker Scores

5 BOUQUET OF FLOWERS

4 LOUD APPLAUSE

3 ENCORE!

2 SLOW HAND CLAP

1 ROTTEN TOMATOES

Best Of The Rest

🔑 The Southwold Summer Theatre puts on a marvellous mix of kids' productions throughout July and August.

Top Tip

The Theatre Royal also organises a summer festival, with floats, fairground rides and fireworks in the nearby Abbey Gardens. Check the website for details.

← The theatre's auditorium

Fascinating Facts

★ **The Bury Theatre Royal is owned by Greene King, a famous local brewery. However, they've given the building to the National Trust on a 999-year lease, so you won't find people brewing beer while you're there!**

★ Theatre folk are very superstitious. All of the following are considered bad luck if taken on stage: real money, real jewellery, peacock feathers, *The Bible*, the colour green and the colour blue (unless countered by wearing silver). And if you want to wish a performer good luck, you should say, 'Break a leg,' (although nobody seems to know why!).

★ **The Theatre of Small Convenience in Worcestershire is believed to be the smallest theatre building in the world. It can seat up to twelve people and is actually a converted Victorian toilet!**

PLAN YOUR VISIT 16

Theatre Royal
5 Westgate Street, Bury St Edmunds, IP33 1QR
www.theatreroyal.org

📞 **01284 769505**

🕐 Tue 14.00, Thu 14.00
Sat 11.00, Sun 11.00

£
££ (for kids' shows)

I want to go here ☐

...at Moyse's Hall

A book's cover should give you an idea of what it is about. At Moyse's Hall you'll see an extreme example of this – a book describing a murder trial that's bound in the criminal's skin!

Moyse's Hall Museum contains artefacts connected with the Red Barn murder. In 1827, a woman called Maria Marten was shot dead by her lover William Corder. Her body was found in the Red Barn near Bury St Edmunds. Corder was tracked down, tried and hanged.

THE BELLY BUTTON BOOK

Sticker Scores

5 CREEPY COVER

4 BLOODTHIRSTY BINDING

3 JITTERY JACKET

2 TERRIBLE TOME

1 VILE VOLUME

When you visit, you'll see a report of the trial which has a cover made from Corder's skin! Also on display are Corder's scalp, ear and death mask (a wax cast of his face made shortly after death). It's a gruesome way to spend a day!

HUMAN SKIN

Best Of The Rest

🔑 Make your own sundial in the clock gallery. Moyse's Hall also has a huge collection of unusual clocks.

🔑 Try brass rubbing. Materials are provided for you to create your own seal of St Edmund, the founder of Bury. (We mean a wax seal by the way – St Edmund was not a marine mammal!)

Make A Day Of It

🔑 Picnic in the gardens of a ruined abbey. A large abbey, housing nuns, used to stand in the centre of Bury. Now there are only ruins, but it's still a great place to run around.

← Be amazed by Moyse's Hall

Fascinating Facts

⭐ **Maria's decomposing head was used as evidence in the trial, as the wounds to her skull showed that she had been shot.**

⭐ The case captured the public's imagination. Thousands wanted to see the Red Barn for themselves. There were over 200,000 visitors during the summer of 1828 alone. The rope used to hang Corder was cut into small sections and sold as souvenirs. We'd rather have a stick of rock . . .

⭐ **Corder's skeleton was donated to West Suffolk hospital. Until the 1940s, it was used to teach nurses about parts of the body. Sometimes they even took it to dances!**

SUFFOLK

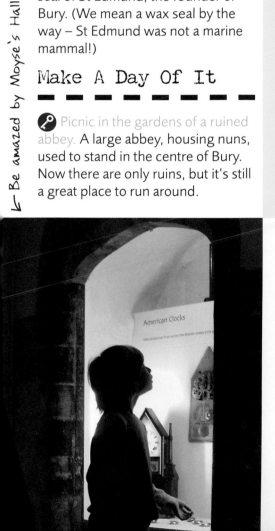

American Clocks

PLAN YOUR VISIT ⓱

Moyse's Hall Museum
Cornhill, Bury St Edmunds, IP33 1DX
www.stedmundsbury.gov.uk

📞 **01284 757160**

🕐 **Daily 10.00-16.00**

£

I want to go here ☐

SCOFF TUDOR SWEETS
...at Kentwell Hall

Tudor monarchs are well-known for executing their enemies. But in amongst the beheadings, they took time out for tea.

Kentwell Hall's Tudor re-creation days show you how a family in a great Tudor house might have lived. Their aim is to re-create the sights, sounds and smells of Tudor life. There's no need for you to come in costume, but the sixteenth-century 'residents' around you will be kitted out in corsets and breeches.

As you walk through the grounds you'll see hunting and dancing. You might even catch a lute concert. Best of all, you'll have the chance to join a banquet, complete with jesters and food fights! The Tudors particularly liked sweet treats, so back then people lost their teeth as well as their heads!

Sticker Scores

5 SUPER SWEET

4 MARVELLOUS MARZIPAN

3 COOL CONFECTIONARY

2 TASTY TREAT

1 TOOTHACHE

Best Of The Rest

🔑 Feed the fish that live in the moat (they're not in costume). Food is available from the entrance.

🔑 Pick up a peacock plume. Peacocks roam the grounds and you can take home any fallen feathers.

🔑 Walk inside a camera. The camera obscura is a small dark building in the grounds, which lets you watch moving images through a hole in the side.

What was the first thing Queen Elizabeth did after she came to the throne?
Sat down!

Fascinating Facts

★ In the 1500s people thought fresh fruit was bad for you. They mainly used it to make jam. So next time you're offered a piece of fruit and don't fancy it, just say you're living like a Tudor!

★ Queen Elizabeth I sucked sugared violets to keep her breath fresh. Sadly for her they also rotted her teeth, so to improve her appearance she filled in the gaps with white cloth.

★ The rich could afford to buy lots of sugar, so they had worse teeth than commoners. Poor people sometimes even painted their teeth black to make it look like they were rich!

SUFFOLK

PLAN YOUR VISIT 18

Kentwell Hall
Long Melford, Sudbury, CO10 9BA
www.kentwell.co.uk
📞 01787 310207
🕐 Daily 11.00-17.00

££

I want to go here ☐

GET LOST IN A VICTORIAN MAZE

...at Somerleyton Hall and Gardens

You may end up spending longer than you planned at Somerleyton. Not just because it's a nice spot, but because the gardens contain a dastardly maze!

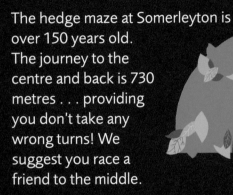

The hedge maze at Somerleyton is over 150 years old. The journey to the centre and back is 730 metres . . . providing you don't take any wrong turns! We suggest you race a friend to the middle.

When (or if) you make it out of the maze, you can tackle several other challenges around Somerleyton. Head over to the adventure playground, or go boating on Fritton Lake. You'll be a-*maze*-d by how much there is to do!

Sticker Scores

5 AMAZING MAZE

4 IMPRESSIVE PRIVET

3 LOONY LABYRINTH

2 BORING BUSH

1 LOST

Similar Spots

 In summer, many farms open maize mazes made of corn. We particularly like the Milton Maize Maze near Cambridge. www.miltonmaizemaze.co.uk

Photo Op

Get someone to take a photo of you on top of the mound at the centre of Somerleyton maze. That way if you never find your way out, at least people will know that you made it to the middle!

"I thought you said to turn left!"

Fascinating Facts

★ Hedge mazes can be incredibly complex creations. For example, the maze at Longleat House in Wiltshire is built on several layers with bridges. And the maze at Hever Castle in Kent now features water jets which squirt explorers who take a wrong turn!

★ The oldest surviving maze in Britain is at Hampton Court, near London. To avoid getting lost you need to put your hand on the nearest wall at the entrance. If you keep your hand against it at all times as you walk you will eventually reach the centre.

★ Mazes aren't the only fun thing you can do with hedges. Topiary is the art of shaping trees and shrubs into sculptures. At Kentwell Hall (see p48) you can run through a yew hedge cut to look like a castle!

SUFFOLK

PLAN YOUR VISIT 19

Somerleyton Hall and Gardens

Lowestoft, NR32 5QQ

www.somerleyton.co.uk

📞 01502 734901

🕐 Thu, Sun & bank holidays 10.00-17.00

£

I want to go here ☐

GO CRABBING

...in Walberswick

Were you born after 1890? If so, you're allowed to enter the British Open Crabbing Championships, which are held on the first Sunday in August in Walberswick!

Crabbing is a simple sport. You just need a line and the bait of your choice (bacon is popular) – no nets or hooks are allowed during the championships – and the person who catches the heaviest crab wins. Competition is fierce and many entrants keep bait recipe a closely guarded secret. The winner receives a gold medal and All entrants receive a crab paste.

Even if you're not in Walberswick during championships, go crabbing off a friend and sh there's no ne

Sticker Scores

5	**4**	**3**
PRIZE CATCH	PERFECT PINCERS	CRACKING CRUSTACEAN
2	**1**	
SHRIVELLED SHRIMP	CRAB APPLE	

↙ Hunting for creatures in Walberswick

Make A Day Of It

🔑 Walk to Southwold. It's a flat, easy route with great views across the reeds (see p54). Look out for boats being repaired in the boatyards.

🔑 Take a high-speed boat trip on the *Sea Blast* – a powerful twelve-seater motorboat. There is also a passenger rowing boat which costs under a pound but takes much longer!

🔑 Watch a classic film at the Electric Picture Palace in Southwold. It's a tiny traditional seaside cinema. An organist plays music before the film starts!

> **Why was the crab sent to prison?**
> **Because he kept pinching things!**

Fascinating Facts

★ **A crab's teeth are located in its stomach. We presume that means crabs can suffer from toothache AND tummy ache at the same time!**

★ If a crab loses a claw it grows back. So if one drops off it's no *claws* for concern!

★ **On average, crabs live for up to three years. However, Japanese spider crabs have been known to live for more than a century!**

★ People in the UK hardly ever live to be over 110, so the Crabbing Championships age restrictions are unlikely to decrease the number of entrants by much.

PLAN YOUR VISIT 20

Walberswick Harbour
Ferry Rd, Walberswick, IP18 6TN
Crabbing Championships: first Sunday in August

£ (championships)
FREE (any other time)

I want to go here ☐

PLAY ARCADE GAMES

...on Southwold Pier

Your parents might moan if you take your PlayStation down to the beach. But even they will have fun playing old-fashioned computer games under the pier in Southwold!

The Under the Pier Show is an alternative arcade full of wacky machines and simulator rides. They're all operated by coins and designed by a local inventor. We particularly like the Booth of Truth, which predicts your future. Also try the Cyclepong machine which lets you play Ping-Pong using pedal power. There's even a magic carpet!

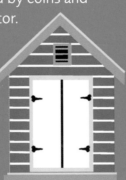

Sticker Scores

5	**4**	**3**
INGENIOUS INVENTION	BRILLIANT BRAINWAVE	MAD MACHINE
2	**1**	
CRAZY CONTRAPTION	IT'LL NEVER WORK	

If you get your own flash of inspiration, you can make suggestions for new gizmos to go in the arcade. The owner always welcomes new ways to get visitors to spend a penny (as in pay money, not have a wee!).

Best Of The Rest

🔑 Watch a clock take a wee. The clock at the end of the pier features mechanical figures, which are powered by water. When the clock strikes the hour, the figures crank into action, dropping their trousers and then squirting each other. *Urine* for a treat!

🔑 Spot a celeb in a shed. Southwold is famous for its rows of brightly coloured beach huts. These days they are very chic sheds. Many are owned by celebrities and sell for thousands of pounds!

🔑 Climb a lighthouse. Trinity Lighthouse saves sailors by night and opens to visitors by day.

← The pier at Southwold

Fascinating Facts

⭐ Early computer and video games were played in coin-operated public arcades rather than at home. The machines were housed in large wooden cabinets that made them look more like pieces of furniture.

⭐ The very first computer game appeared in 1971 and was called Computer Space. It was a flop, but its creators persisted and later launched Pong (as in Ping-Pong, not a bad smell!). That was far more successful and inspired the modern computer-game industry.

Photo Op
Step inside the Expressive Photo Booth. It's a camera corner with a twist! The seat might suddenly drop or gusts of air blow in your face.

PLAN YOUR VISIT 21

Under the Pier Show
Southwold Pier, IP18 6BN
www.underthepier.com

📞 01502 7221055

🕐 Daily (peak) 10.00-19.00
Daily (out of season) 10.00-17.00

I want to go here ☐

ROW OUT TO A PIRATE'S LAIR

...at the Thorpeness Meare

You don't have to cross the Caribbean to reach a pirate's island! There are bays and coves a-plenty on the boating lake at Thorpeness.

Thorpeness is a remarkable holiday village that was built by a curious chap called Stuart Ogilvie. Stuart decided that the area was a perfect holiday destination . . . so in the early 1900s he built a bunch of houses, a lake (the Meare) and some tiny islands here. We reckon you'll be particularly impressed by the Pirate's Lair – because we *aaaarr*!!

There are many ways to look around the lake – you can rent rowing boats, canoes or pedalos. In our opinion, Thorpeness is a modern day *Meare*-acle!

Sticker Scores

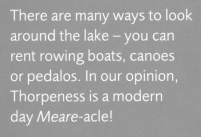

5 — SHIP SHAPE

4 — ROCKING ROW BOAT

3 — CANNY CANOE

2 — DINGY DINGHY

1 — PEDAL-O DEAR!

Make A Day Of It

🔑 **Be amazed by the House in the Clouds**, which overlooks the Thorpeness Meare. This architectural curiosity is a house built on top of a water tower. It looks like it's floating above the trees!

🔑 **Check out the large scallop-shell sculpture** on the beach at Aldeburgh.

🔑 **Chomp on some cracking fish and chips** at The Fish And Chip Shop on Aldeburgh High Street. We think they serve the best fish and chips in East Anglia.

Why does Peter Pan always fly?

Because he can *Neverland*!

Fascinating Facts

⭐ **The Ogilvie family were not just cuddly island creators. They were also well known for killing birds and stuffing them! Some are still on display at Ipswich Museum.**

⭐ Ogilvie was inspired to make a mystical holiday land by his friend J.M. Barrie – the author of *Peter Pan*. Many of the places at Thorpeness have names that refer to the book, like the Pirate's Lair and Wendy's Place.

⭐ **One of the most popular monuments in London is the Peter Pan statue in Kensington Gardens. It was put up secretly in the night on May 1st 1912 – so many people assumed it had appeared by magic!**

PLAN YOUR VISIT 22

The Thorpeness Meare

Remembrance Road, Aldringham, Thorpeness, IP16 4NW

www.themeareatthorpeness.com

📞 01728 832523

££

I want to go here ☐

WALK TO A SECRET LIGHTHOUSE

...at Orford Ness

Usually a lighthouse can be seen for miles around. But for many years, only sailors and spies knew about the lighthouse at Orford Ness.

Orford Ness is a long strip of land that extends ten miles into the sea. The area is an uninhabited nature reserve and there is no direct access from the mainland. During the twentieth century it was used by the military as a secret testing site for radar and nuclear weapons! The lighthouse was only switched on in special circumstances.

A boat service from the town of Orford now allows you to explore the ness on foot. Follow the trail past the old broadcasting aerials and out to the lighthouse. And don't worry – these days you're allowed to tell people you're visiting!

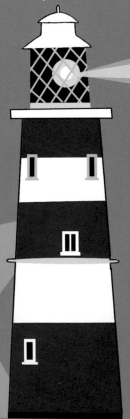

Sticker Scores

5 RESCUE RAY

4 BOLD BEAM

3 FOG LIGHT

2 BIG LAMP

1 ROTATING TORCH

Make A Day Of It

🔑 Investigate a UFO landing site. Nearby Rendelsham Forest is the site of one of Britain's most famous UFO events. Pick up a UFO trail map from the forest centre.

🔑 Hear the bells of a drowning town. Coastal erosion means that the village of Dunwich is slipping into the sea at the rate of one metre per year. You can find out more in the Dunwich Museum.

← "It's behind you!"

What's the difference between a lighthouse keeper and a jeweller?

One watches seas, and the other sees watches.

Fascinating Facts

⭐ **Orford Ness was also home to a Cold War spying operation known as Cobra Mist. In the 1960s the Americans constructed a huge steel building at the north end of the ness to monitor Russian and Chinese aircraft. It was abandoned in 1973 and is now used by the BBC World Service to transmit radio programmes to Eastern Europe.**

⭐ The first ever message in a bottle was thrown out to sea in 1776 by Henry Whiteside, the builder of Smalls Lighthouse in Wales. Stranded on an island with his crew, Henry tossed his message to the waves. It sailed to shore and the crew were rescued!

SUFFOLK

PLAN YOUR VISIT 23

Orford Ness Nature Reserve

Quay Office, Orford Quay, Orford, Woodbridge, IP12 2NU

www.nationaltrust.org.uk

📞 **01728 648024**

🕐 **Tue-Sat (peak) 10.00-14.00**
Sat (out of season) 10.00-14.00

££

I want to go here ☐

BRAVE THE BATTLEMENTS

...at Framlingham Castle

If you'd visited Framlingham Castle 500 years ago, walking the battlements would not have been a good idea. Unless, that is, you fancied getting shot by an arrow!

Framlingham Castle is unusual because unlike most medieval castles it has no keep (that's the stronghold in the middle). Instead, it relied on one very tall, very thick wall with four towers that contained all the domestic buildings. This meant that when the castle was under attack the action took place on the battlements at the top of the wall.

Today you can climb the towers and walk along the wall. Peer through the slits from where the archers fired arrows and imagine you're defending the castle from enemy invaders . . .

Sticker Scores

⭐ 5 — KNIGHT IN SHINING ARMOUR

⭐ 4 — AWESOME ARCHER

⭐ 3 — SKILFUL SQUIRE

⭐ 2 — CRUEL CROSSBOWMAN

⭐ 1 — KNIGHT IN RUSTY ARMOUR

Who invented King Arthur's round table?

Sir Cumference!

Make A Day Of It

🔑 Explore Orford Castle, another great castle that's nearby. However, unlike its neighbour, Framlingham, it has a cracking keep and no outer wall. Falconry displays also regularly take place in the grounds.

🔑 See how to smoke meat at Richardson's Smokehouse in Orford. Before people had fridges this was one way they made food last longer. You'll smell the smokehouse from a long way off!

Photo Op

Get a snap of you crouching like a crossbowman and looking through the castle's arrow slits.

Fascinating Facts

⭐ During the Middle Ages, Framlingham was owned by a family of scheming knights called the Bigods. They used their base at Framlingham to challenge the king and other noble families. Unsurprisingly, the castle was attacked many times.

⭐ A disgraced knight could have his spurs (the spikes on his boots) hacked off and his shield hung upside down as punishment.

⭐ Fighting on piggyback was an important part of training for young knights! It was a simple way to introduce them to the skills required in full combat, without having to bring in a real horse.

← Framlingham Castle

SUFFOLK

PLAN YOUR VISIT 24

Framlingham Castle

Framlingham, Suffolk, IP13 9BP

www.english-heritage.org.uk

📞 01728 724189

🕐 Daily (peak) 10.00-18.00
Daily (out of season) 10.00-16.00

£ 🎁

I want to go here ☐

...at Sutton Hoo

Nowadays people make wills which explain what they want to happen to their possessions after they die. However, 1,000 years ago, your best belongings were often buried with you.

Sutton Hoo is a treasure trove of Saxon objects. Local people had long told stories about the mysterious mounds near the river Deben and when archaeologists finally excavated in 1939 they uncovered a magnificent series of burial chambers.

The most famous discovery is what is thought to be the grave of King Raedwald. This warrior-king was buried in his ship along with his swords, armour and a terrifying spiked helmet. You can walk round the tomb of this former royal yacht and marvel at artefacts in the visitor centre. The site has now been dug many times for more treasure, so leave your metal detector at home!

RIP
" SHIP "

Sticker Scores

5
BURIED
BOUNTY

4
TUCKED-AWAY
TREASURE

3
LOST
LOOT

2
RUSTY
COINS

1
TIN
FOIL

WAS BURIED

Make A Day Of It

 Curl up with a book in Young Browsers Bookshop in Woodbridge. It's another kind of treasure trove!

 Try a new water sport at Bawdsey Quay. Kayaking, powerboarding and laser sailing are all on offer. Those who prefer dry land can hire bikes.

Why was the archaeologist such a failure? Because his career lay in ruins!

← Anglo-Saxon armour at Sutton Hoo

Fascinating Facts

★ **King Raedwald was buried with five thrusting spears and three throwing spears. There was also a long-handled axe-hammer to give an enemy a very sore head!**

★ Buried treasure doesn't have to be shiny. According to the 1996 Treasure Act, any object that contains at least ten per cent of precious metal and is over 300 years old qualifies as treasure. Items that are made mostly of gold and silver where the original owners cannot be traced can also be defined as treasure.

★ **More buried treasure is unearthed in Norfolk than in any other county in the UK. Bear this in mind when you're out exploring some of the other sites in this book!**

SUFFOLK

PLAN YOUR VISIT 25

Sutton Hoo
Tranmer House, Sutton Hoo, Woodbridge, IP12 3DJ
www.suttonhoo.org

📞 01394 389700

🕐 **Daily (peak) 10.30-17.00**
Daily (out of season) Sat-Sun 11.00-16.00

££

I want to go here ☐

PAMPER A RACEHORSE

...at the Newmarket National Stud

We all like to look our best before a special occasion, and racehorses have a lot of big days out. When you visit Newmarket, you can help to keep them in tip-top condition.

Newmarket is the headquarters of British horse racing. The town is home to two racecourses, several training yards and all the key horse-racing organisations. It is also the location of the National Stud, the largest breeding centre for thoroughbreds (a particularly speedy breed of racehorse).

Tours of the stud give you a chance to see behind the stable door. You can groom and brush one of the stallions or treat the ponies to a polo mint. It's a galloping good day out!

Sticker Scores

5 HEROIC HORSE

4 FAST FOAL

3 PLEASANT PONY

2 MUNDANE MULE

1 SILLY ASS

Best Of The Rest

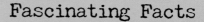

 Dress up as a jockey. The National Horseracing Museum in Newmarket is full of racing memorabilia, including skeletons of former champs (the horses, not the riders!). In the Practical Gallery you can dress up in a jockey's outfit and ride a racing-horse simulator.

 Spend a day at the races. To see the thoroughbreds in action, go to the Newmarket racecourse. Look out for the family race day in July, which features a whole host of extra equine entertainments.

← See if you can pick a winner

Why did the pony have to gargle?

Because it was a little *hoarse*!

Fascinating Facts

★ **Over one million thoroughbred foals are born worldwide each year. Astonishingly, all can trace their ancestry back to one of three horses.**

★ Remember the following rules if you ever see a statue of a soldier sitting on a horse . . . If the horse has both front legs in the air, it usually means the person died in battle. If the horse has one front leg in the air, the person died as a result of wounds received in battle. If the horse has all four legs on the ground, the person died of natural causes.

★ **Horses can produce as much as nine tonnes of manure each year. That's the equivalent of six small cars (but much more smelly)!**

PLAN YOUR VISIT 26

The National Stud
Newmarket, CB8 0XE
www.nationalstud.co.uk

📞 01638 663464

🕐 Tours daily (peak): 11.15 & 14.00 (booking essential)

££

I want to go here ☐

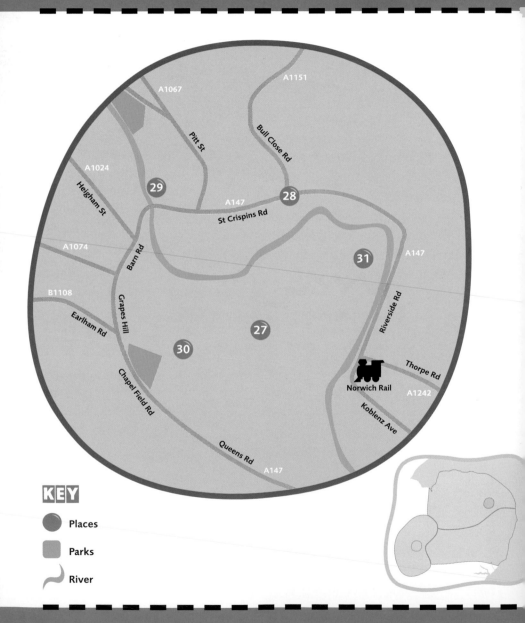

A1151

A1067

Pitt St

Bull Close Rd

A1024

Heigham St

29

A147

St Crispins Rd

28

A1074

Barn Rd

31

A147

B1108

Grapes Hill

Riverside Rd

Earlham Rd

27

Chapel Field Rd

30

Norwich Rail

Thorpe Rd

A1242

Koblenz Ave

Queens Rd

A147

KEY

● Places

▬ Parks

〜 River

CAMBRIDGE

CAMBRIDGESHIRE

SUFFOLK

NORWICH

NORFOLK

TOP FIVES

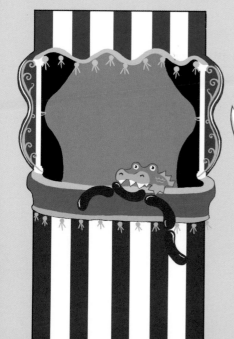

SEE THE WORLD'S LARGEST COLLECTION

...at Norwich Castle

Norwich castle was built to defend the city against enemy invasion. So it might seem a surprising place to enjoy a nice cup of tea!

The castle was built by William the Conqueror, at a time when the Norman rulers faced many local rebellions. Nowadays it holds objects from all periods of history – including the world's largest collection of ceramic teapots!

There are over 3,000 teapots in the Twining Teapot Gallery. They come in all sorts of shapes – there's a war tank, a cabbage, a castle, a pineapple and even a monkey. You'll also find teapots of all sizes, from *tea*-ny teapots no higher than your finger to giant ones longer than your arm! Pre-*tea* amazing!

Sticker Scores

5 MY CUP OF TEA

4 PERFECT POT

3 CHARMING CHINA

2 COLD CUPPA

1 *POUR* SHOW

Best Of The Rest

🔑 Take a tour of the dungeons. The castle used to include a prison, so book a dungeon tour to see gruesome instruments of torture and plaster casts of criminals' heads!

🔑 Watch a play in a moat. The Whiffler Theatre is a small open-air theatre in the castle moat. (Don't worry; there isn't even a re-*moat* chance of flooding!)

Similar Spots

🔑 Castle Rising near King's Lynn is another excellent example of a Norman Castle. (We don't mean a castle called Norman, but a castle built by the Normans!)

← Not a teapot!

Fascinating Facts

⭐ **According to popular legend, tea was first discovered by the Chinese Emperor Shen Nung when a few leaves fell off a tea bush into a pot in which he was boiling water.**

⭐ After water, tea is the most popular beverage in the world.

⭐ **Tea was first drunk in England in public coffee houses during the 1600s. These places were for men; women could only drink tea in their own homes.**

⭐ Pirates were not only interested in finding gold and treasure. High taxes on tea in the late 1700s meant that a boatload of tea was a valuable haul!

PLAN YOUR VISIT (27)

Norwich Castle
Castle Meadow, Norwich, NR1 3JU
www.museums.norfolk.gov.uk

📞 **01603 493625**

🕐 **Mon-Sat (peak) 10.00-17.00
Sun (peak) 13.00-17.00
Mon-Sat (out of season) 10.00-16.30
Sun (out of season 13.00-16.30**

I want to go here ☐

PUT ON A PUPPET SHOW

...at Norwich Puppet Theatre

If you want to stage your own play, you need performers you can trust. And since actors sometimes throw tantrums, we suggest you use entertainers that will always do exactly what you want – puppets!

Norwich Puppet Theatre is located inside an abandoned church. They run regular puppet-making workshops, each themed around a particular type of puppet. Working with a professional, you make the basic puppet and are then free to give it the style, character and decoration you want.

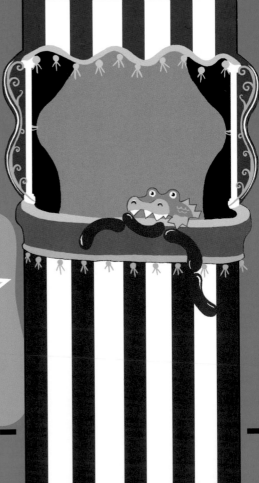

You can also book to see performances by puppet companies from all across the world. It's a great experience – with no strings attached!

Sticker Scores

5 PERFECT PUPPET

4 MARVELLOUS MARIONETTE

3 DESIGNER DOLL

2 CARDBOARD CUT-OUT

1 SMELLY SOCK

← Dancing puppets

Photo Op

Get a cast photo of you and your puppet. If it's a glove puppet, stand behind a table or counter so that your arm is hidden.

Why are glove puppets more successful than marionettes?

Because they've all got a hand up!

Top Tip

The theatre's Adopt-A-Puppet club lets you support a puppet once its performing days are over! Look out for photos of puppets up for adoption inside the theatre.

Fascinating Facts

★ A marionette is a type of string puppet. The word means 'Little Mary' in French, and comes from the fact that in France it was once against the law for a real actor to play a character from *The Bible*. String puppets were therefore used to represent people like the Virgin Mary.

★ Ventriloquism is the art of making your voice sound like it is coming from a dummy (a form of puppet, not a silly person!). The trick is to speak without using your lips. That's surprisingly easy for many sounds (try it!). However, the letters B, P, V, M and W all require a lot of lip movement, so are much harder to do.

 **PLAN YOUR VISIT** 28

Norwich Puppet Theatre
St James, Whitefriars, Norwich, NR3 1TN
www.puppettheatre.co.uk

📞 01603 615564

🕐 Daily 09.30-17.00

££ 🍴 🎁 ☂

I want to go here ☐

NORWICH

71

GET STRUCK BY LIGHTNING

...at Inspire Discovery Centre

Getting struck by lightning doesn't sound much fun. In fact, it sounds very painful! Fortunately the lightning at the Inspire Discovery Centre is contained within a large glass ball, so you're unlikely to be frazzled to death!

Inspire is a hands-on science museum. There are over 30 interactive experiments, which let you do things like shake hands with yourself, spin plates or even build a balloon-powered buggy!

We particularly like the plasma ball. When you touch this globe, a spark of electricity flows up towards your hand and over your body surface to earth. It's like being struck by lightning, but the amount of energy produced is far lower than in a real thunderstorm. And you can try the experiment again and again . . . so sometimes lightning does strike twice!

Sticker Scores

5 EXCELLENT EXPERIMENT

4 SUPER SPARK

3 BRILLIANT BOLT

2 FANTASTIC FLASH

1 ELECTRIC SHOCK

Best Of The Rest

 Step inside a bubble. The world record for the number of people inside a bubble is 25, and it was set at the Inspire Discovery Centre in 2008. You too can step inside a bubble during your visit. Stand on the platform and pull the giant hoop of bubble mixture over your head.

Photo Op

Photograph your shadow. Don't worry if you've forgotten your camera. Jump in the Inspire light box and take a shadow photograph. Make a star shape and your outline will appear on the wall!

Fascinating Facts

★ *Guinness World Records* lists an American called Roy Sullivan as the human being to have been struck by lightning the most times. With seven shocks to his name, this is one record you definitely don't want to beat!

★ Experts recommend the 30/30 rule for staying safe in a thunderstorm. As soon as you see lightning, count the seconds until you hear thunder. If the number is 30 seconds or less, seek shelter. Then stay under cover until 30 minutes after the last thunder clap or visible lightning flash.

Where does bad light end up?
In a prism!

← A shocking sight

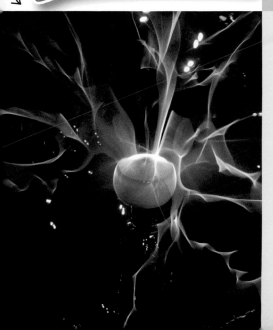

PLAN YOUR VISIT 29

Inspire Discovery Centre
St Michael's Church, Oak Street, Norwich, NR3 3AE
www.inspirediscoverycentre.com

📞 **01603 612612**

🕐 **Mon-Fri 10.00-16.00**
Sat-Sun 11.00-17.00

I want to go here ☐

NORWICH

73

BECOME A TV PRESENTER

...at BBC East

Ever watched a TV presenter and thought, *I could do that*? Well, at the BBC studios in Norwich you can finally have a go!

The BBC East studios broadcast all regional TV and radio programmes for the east of England. The behind-the-scenes studio tour shows you the kinds of things that you don't see on screen. Because programmes are being filmed as you walk round, the tour might be re-routed at any moment – but we think this just adds to the excitement!

Sticker Scores

⭐ 5 — **BIG SCREEN**

⭐ 4 — **FLAT SCREEN**

⭐ 3 — **WIDE SCREEN**

⭐ 2 — **SMALL SCREEN**

⭐ 1 — **BIG SCREAM**

You will see how a studio works, examine an editing suite and even handle the cameras. Then comes your chance for a screen test, where you can read the news or the weather. Don't forget to say, 'Hi, Mum'!

Similar Spots

 Head to Cinema City to watch fun films on a big screen. It's an independent cinema, with three screens inside a medieval merchant's house. Check out their weekly kids' club.

Photo Op

If you bump into one of the real newsreaders, ask nicely for a photo with one of them – they're used to smiling for the camera!

← Inside BBC Norwich

Fascinating Facts

★ The BBC is the largest broadcasting organisation in the world, and employs over 20,000 people. That's about the same number of people as you'd find living in a small town!

★ The first television programme especially for kids was broadcast in 1936. It was shown once a week and was only ten minutes long. So in those days you would have rarely been told off for watching too much TV!

★ A British designer called Stuart Hughes has made the world's most expensive television set. It's worth £1.5 million, and is made using 28 kilogrammes of solid gold, 72 diamonds and hand-sewn alligator skin. We think it's a rather *snappy* design!

PLAN YOUR VISIT 30

BBC East Studios

The Forum, Millennium Plain, Norwich, NR2 1BH

www.bbc.co.uk/tours

📞 0370 901 1227

🕐 Sun 10.15, 13.00, 14.45 (advance booking only)

££ ☂

I want to go here ☐

PROMENADE WITH THE PARANORMAL

...on the Norwich ghost walk

Norwich is a medieval city with many murky secrets. Residents have reported strange sights in the old parts. With a torch and some sturdy shoes you can try to find out the truth behind the tales.

On the Norwich ghost walk, your guide (known as the Man in Black) will lead you through the winding alleys and cobbled streets. Here you will be told tales of mad priests, plague victims, witches, headless horses and much more.

A supremely spooky part of the city is the area known as Tombland. This is where the gruesome Black Death struck in the 1300s. So perhaps there really are ghostly goings-on. Wrap up warm, keep close together and you should return in high *spirits*!

Sticker Scores

5 FANTASTIC PHANTOM

4 GLORIOUS GHOST

3 GLOOMY GHOUL

2 SURLY SPECTRE

1 SHEET OVER HEAD

Similar Spots

 Blickling Hall in Norfolk was recently voted the most haunted house in Britain by the National Trust! It was the home of Anne Boleyn, the second wife of Henry VIII, who was beheaded. It is said that every year, on the anniversary of her execution, Anne Boleyn's headless ghost arrives at Blickling Hall in a carriage driven by an equally headless coachman.

Why are graveyards so noisy?
Because of all the *coffin'*!

← *Whhoooooooo!*

Fascinating Facts

★ **The Black Death is the name given to a particularly nasty outbreak of plague in the 1300s. It was especially devastating for the people of Norwich – in 1362 one third of the town died from the disease.**

★ One of the most frequently reported ghost sightings in Norwich is the Grey Girl, who treads the floorboards of Steward House and the Tombland alleyway. In 1578 another outbreak of the plague killed the occupants of this building and it was boarded up for several weeks. Unfortunately a young girl in the house had survived, but trapped inside and unable to escape, she slowly starved to death.

NORWICH

PLAN YOUR VISIT 31

Ghost Walks Norwich
Adam and Eve pub, Bishopsgate, Norwich, NR3 1RZ (start point)
www.ghostwalksnorwich.co.uk
📞 07831 189985
🕐 Mon-Thu 19.30
£

I want to go here ☐

NORFOLK

Burnham Overy — 41

37 — Hunstanton

Wells-next-the-Sea — 39

42 — Cromer

A148

44

36

Fakenham — 43

North Walsham

40

A140

32

33

King's Lynn

A148

A1065

A47

A47

Swaffham

Norwich

A47

Great Yarmouth

The Broads — 45

A134

38

A1065

Wymondham

Attleborough

34

Brandon — 35

Thetford

A11

KEY

Places

CAMBRIDGE

CAMBRIDGESHIRE

SUFFOLK

NORWICH

NORFOLK

TOP FIVES

STEER A MOTOR CRUISER

...on the Norfolk Broads

Boating is the number-one activity on the Norfolk Broads – guided boat trips run all year round. However, we think it's heaps more fun to hire your own ship and take charge of the wheel!

The broads cover a vast area of channels, lakes and rivers. For centuries, buildings have been constructed facing the water rather than the roads. This means the best views are from the river. There are no tides and the water is shallow, so it's a perfect place for first-time sailors!

You'll see boat-hire companies all over the broads. We like Whispering Reeds near Hickling. Ask for the *Bittern*, a little motor cruiser which can be rented out for half a day. All a-*broad*!

Sticker Scores

5	4	3
FLEET ADMIRAL	SHIP'S CAPTAIN	FIRST MATE

2	1
ABLE SEAMAN	STOWAWAY

Top Tip
Take some stale bread with you to feed the many ducks that live on the broads.

Best Of The Rest

🔑 **Canoe up a creek** and see the secret backwaters of the broads. The Canoe Man runs kayak trails and treasure hunts. www.thecanoeman.com

🔑 **Board a solar-powered boat.** The *Ra* is named after the Egyptian sun god and is Britain's first solar-powered boat. www.tournorfolk.co.uk

🔑 **Go yachting.** The beautiful wooden yachts available from Hunter's yard at Ludham are also environmentally friendly, but a lot more low tech. www.huntersyard.co.uk

Fascinating Facts

⭐ **The Norfolk Broads look natural, but they are in fact man-made. In the Middle Ages, the area was dug for peat (a fuel a bit like coal). The surrounding rivers flooded and water seeped into the area, forming new lakes.**

⭐ The whole broads area consists of six rivers and 63 lakes.

⭐ **They may have formed by accident, but nowadays the broads are much loved. In 1988, they were given National Park status, which means they are protected from development. So you'll still be able to go sailing here for years to come!**

← *Swans also like the Norfolk Broads!*

PLAN YOUR VISIT 32

Whispering Reeds
Staithe Rd, Hickling, NR12 0YW
www.whisperingreeds.net
📞 01692 598314

£££

I want to go here ☐

NORFOLK

SWING FROM TREE TO TREE

...at Bewilderwood

If you've ever been told that you're a bit of a monkey, you'll love the tree-swinging antics at Bewilderwood. It's a _tree_-mendous experience!

Bewilderwood is a tree-top adventure playground spread over 50 acres of forest and marshland. The park is based on a series of brilliant books by local author Tom Blofeld. You can see some of the weird and wonderful characters from his stories in the woods.

A boat ride across the swamp takes you into the heart of Bewilderwood. Aerial walkways, rope tunnels and zip wires connect painted tree houses to one another. The quickest way to get back to the ground is down the Slippery Slope slide, which has a drop of twenty metres. We're sure you _wood_ not want to miss it!

Sticker Scores

5 TOP TREE

4 BLOSSOMING TREE

3 CHRISTMAS TREE

2 FAMILY TREE

1 MUG TREE

Similar Spots

🔑 Bump into a brontosaurus at the Dinosaur Adventure Park. A T-Rex and Pterodactyls (or at least life-size models of them) also lurk in this monster woodland.

🔑 Exercise a ferret on the farm at Wroxham Barns. You can also bottle-feed baby lambs, play a round of mini golf and satisfy your sweet tooth in the fudge shop.

Top Tip

Stick your neck out and try an unusual ostrich burger at the Bewilderwood snack bar.

← Crossing a rope bridge

Fascinating Facts

⭐ **The world's largest all-wood tree house is in the grounds of Alnwick Castle in Northumberland. It contains toilets, shops and even a 120-seat restaurant!**

⭐ Tree houses have become an important part of many environmental protests. Tree sitting (refusing to move from a den in a tree) has been used in protests against plans to build roads or cut down areas of forest.

⭐ **Julia Butterfly Hill is a well-known tree sitter who occupied a large pine tree in California for nearly two years between 1997 and 1999. She lived on a couple of small platforms twenty metres above the ground and exercised by climbing up and down the trunk. We think she must have been *bark*-ing mad by the time she came down!**

PLAN YOUR VISIT 33

Bewilderwood
Horning Rd, Hoveton, NR12 8JW
www.bewilderwood.co.uk

📞 01603 783900

🕙 Daily (peak) 10.00-17.30

I want to go here ☐

NORFOLK

PEDAL THROUGH A PINE FOREST

...at Thetford

Thetford forest is the largest lowland forest in the UK. It is also one of the driest spots in the country. And all this makes it perfect territory to go exploring on two wheels.

The forest is crisscrossed with walking and cycling tracks. There are four coloured biking routes; from the gentle green for beginners to the very difficult black trail. Bikes can be hired from Bike Art at the High Lodge Forest Centre.

On your ride you will pedal past pine trees and all types of wildlife. The forest is home to several species of deer and snakes, so be careful not to run them over – that would be a *wheely* bad idea!

Sticker Scores

⭐ 5 — TOP GEAR

⭐ 4 — PEDAL POWER

⭐ 3 — PUMPED UP

⭐ 2 — SLOW PUNCTURE

⭐ 1 — ON YER BIKE

Make A Day Of It

🔑 Feed the giraffes at Banham Zoo. Banham has everything from armadillos to zebras (with lots of monkeys in between). The large open-plan design means that the animals are well cared for. We suggest you board the little train (it stops at the adventure playground too)!

🔑 Swing from tree to tree on the awesome Go Ape forest obstacle course, which is also in Thetford Forest. Age restrictions apply.

What do you call a bike with a degree?
A uni-cycle!

Fascinating Facts

⭐ **The British Siberian Husky Racing Association sometimes holds events in the forest. Husky dogs pull along competitors, who stand on a sleigh with wheels. Sadly though, sleighs are not available for hire!**

⭐ Thetford is overrun with rabbits. Warrens (huge rabbit homes) were set up by humans in the Middle Ages to breed rabbits that would provide food and fur. At the height of the industry there were up to 800,000 rabbits in the area – four times the human population of Thetford today! The number of rabbits has decreased since then, but you should still spot plenty hopping about.

← Tree-mendous!

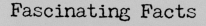 **PLAN YOUR VISIT** 34

Bike Art

High Lodge Forest Centre, Thetford Forest, IP27 0AF
www.forestry.gov.uk/thetfordforestpark

📞 01842 810090

🕐 **Daily (summer) 09.00-18.00**
Daily (out of season) 09.00-16.00

££

I want to go here ☐

NORFOLK

GO DOWN A PREHISTORIC MINE

...at Grime's Graves

This site has nothing to do with dirt or burials. The Grime in question was actually a Saxon god, and at that time the word grave simply meant hole.

Grime's Graves is a flint mine from the Neolithic period (5,000 years ago). Flint is a hard rock that Neolithic men used to make tools like axe heads. The area around the mine is covered in ridges and craters – it looks a bit like the surface of the moon!

One mine shaft is open to visitors. You go down nine metres by ladder and walk to viewing galleries from where you can see the gleaming black flint. There are also demonstrations of flint knapping (making tools from flint). We're glad that these days we can just pop to a hardware shop!

Sticker Scores

5 MARVELLOUS MINE

4 TREMENDOUS TRENCH

3 STANDARD SHAFT

2 QUEER QUARRY

1 LANDMINE

Make A Day Of It

 Mug up on mummies at Swaffham Museum, just north of Thetford. Thetford was the birthplace of Howard Carter, the archaeologist who discovered the tomb of Tutankhamen (an Egyptian pharaoh). The museum has a special exhibition dedicated to his works.

 Zoom down a flume at Breckland Leisure Centre and Waterworld. We love the rolling rapids and wicked water cannon!

What kind of music do cavemen like?
Rock music!

A birds-eye view of Grime's Graves →

Fascinating Facts

★ **Neolithic miners did their digging using picks made from the antlers of red deer.**

★ The miners also had clever ways of getting light underground. They would make lamps by scooping a hole out of a lump of chalk and filling it with animal fat. You can still see soot stains left on the roofs of the galleries by the burning oil from lamps.

★ **Strangely, no remains of food or pottery vessels have been found in the mines. This suggests that the miners climbed out to take their meal breaks in the fresh air!**

★ One of the pits was turned into a shrine by Neolithic miners. They built a small altar and prayed for more flint.

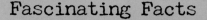

PLAN YOUR VISIT 35

Grime's Graves
Lynford, Nr Thetford, IP26 5DE
www.english-heritage.org.uk

📞 01842 810656

🕐 **Daily (peak) 10.00-18.00**
Thu-Mon (Mar & Oct) 10.00-17.00
Closed Nov-Feb

£

I want to go here ☐

PLAY ON THE QUEEN'S ADVENTURE

...at Sandringham

OK, we admit we haven't actually *seen* the Queen on the swings at Sandringham. But waving at crowds must get boring. And this adventure playground is basically in her back garden.

Sandringham is one of the royal family's country homes – they go there every Christmas. When they're away, the house is open to the public. Inside, you can see many fascinating royal objects, from exotic pearls to the clock used to time Her Majesty's racing pigeons.

Sticker Scores

5 PRINCE'S PLAYGROUND

4 KING'S SWING

3 QUEEN'S CLIMBING FRAME

2 MAID'S MERRY-GO-ROUND

1 PAUPER'S PLAYGROUND

The house is set amidst 60 acres of woodland. Follow the forest trails and then test out the awesome adventure playground. You'll have a right royal time!

← The Queen's home at Sandringham

Best Of The Rest

 Go to jail at King's Lynn Gaol House. A guide will lead you through the old 1930s police station and into dark, smelly cells, which once housed smugglers and highwaymen. You can also learn how witches were identified.

 Take a ferry across King's Lynn's historic waterfront. This old-fashioned boat with a canvas awning is not a high-tech ride, but it's a *ferry* good way to see the town!

 Watch speedway at the Norfolk Arena. Speedway is a motorcycle track sport. It's huge in this region and the Lynn Stars are one of the most successful British speedway teams.

Fascinating Facts

★ **The Queen spends Christmas at Sandringham and summer at her house in Balmoral, in Scotland. Presumably she prefers the warmer winters down here in Norfolk!**

★ The staff at Sandringham keep photos of all the cabinets in the palace. This means that when they remove their contents for dusting, they can put things back precisely where they were before.

When does a prince get wet?
When he becomes the *raining* monarch!

PLAN YOUR VISIT 36

Sandringham House, Museum and Gardens

Sandringham Estate, Sandringham, PE35 6EB
www.sandringhamestate.co.uk

 01353 612908

 Daily (Peak) 10.30-17.00

££

I want to go here ☐

NORFOLK

SUPPORT RESCUED SEA LIFE

...at the Hunstanton Sea Life Sanctuary

You wouldn't normally choose to have a day out in a hospital. However, this sanctuary is a hospital for animals, which means the patients are really cute!

The Hunstanton Sea Life Sanctuary rescues and cares for sick or injured penguins, seals and otters. Some turn up at the sanctuary in a very bad condition, and a special team of vets often has to work through the night just to keep new arrivals alive. The goal is to nurse the animals to health and then release them back into the wild.

Inside the sanctuary you can watch the marine creatures on the road to recovery. We particularly like the otter enclosure, where you can see these playful water weasels fetch fish and frolic in the sun. *Wat-er* great way to spend a day!

Sticker Scores

Best Of The Rest

Come face to face with a stingray. There's also an aquarium at the Sea Life Sanctuary. You are separated by just a wall of glass from stingrays, sharks and sea horses!

Make A Day Of It

Ride a donkey along the beach at Hunstanton (or Sunny Hunny, as it is affectionately known to the locals).

Laugh in Britain's largest joke shop. World of Fun in Hunstaton sells more than 4,000 wigs, masks and whoopee cushions. The shop's owner is the proud inventor of something called The Fart Spray!

← Hunstanton has seals too!

Fascinating Facts

★ **Two thirds of Earth is covered by water that is more than 100 metres deep. However, we know little about these deep seas. Scientists have better maps of the moon's surface than they have of the ocean floor!**

★ Otters were once quite common in Britain until habitat loss and pollution caused their numbers to decline over the past 50 years. Thanks to sanctuaries like Hunstanton the otter population has recently begun to show signs of recovery. To celebrate, we've put an otter on the front of this book!

★ **Stingrays produce a venom that can be deadly to humans. So you wouldn't want to come face to face with one in the wild!**

PLAN YOUR VISIT 37

Hunstanton Sea Life Sanctuary
Southern Promenade, Hunstanton, PE36 5BH
www.sealsanctuary.co.uk

 01485 53376

Daily 10.00-16.00

 ££

I want to go here ☐

NORFOLK

CRAWL INSIDE A HIDING HOLE

...at Oxburgh Hall

Nowadays we play hide-and-seek for fun, but in the sixteenth century, priests sometimes had to find really good hiding places to keep themselves alive!

Oxburgh Hall is a grand Tudor home with a massive moat. It was owned by a family of Catholics at a time when it was forbidden to be a Catholic in England. The family helped to hide priests whose lives were at risk. They created secret chambers beneath floorboards and behind walls for priests to crawl into during a royal raid.

There are many priest-holes around the country, but Oxburgh is one of the few which you can still go into today! The hole is reached via a trap door and a very steep ladder. So make sure you have enough energy to climb out after!

Sticker Scores

5 — CUNNING CUBBYHOLE

4 — BRILLIANT BURROW

3 — CANNY CRANNY

2 — NIFTY NOOK

1 — DODGY DEN

Make A Day Of It

🔑 Climb a wind turbine at the Ecotech Centre in Swaffham. 305 steps take you up to the viewing platform.

🔑 Catch sight of a kingfisher at Gooderstone Water Gardens. When a farmer found that his fields were too damp for cattle he turned them into an aquatic treasure trail. Now, thirteen bridges connect streams and ponds brimming with birds, fish and water boatmen (that's a type of insect, not a man in a boat!).

> **Why can't leopards play hide-and-seek?**
>
> Because they are always *spotted*!

← Young warriors at Oxburgh Hall

Fascinating Facts

⭐ **The Protestant search parties who hunted down Catholic priests in the 1500s included carpenters and masons. They tested the walls to work out if there was a secret chamber behind them.**

⭐ One search party received a tip-off that a priest was hidden in a hole behind a fireplace. They couldn't find the entrance so they ordered logs and lit the fire. The priest was burned alive.

⭐ **Oxburgh Hall is a popular location for shooting films and TV programmes. So if you hang around for long enough you might get caught on camera!**

PLAN YOUR VISIT 38

Oxburgh Hall
Oxborough, King's Lynn, PE33 9PS
www.nationaltrust.org.uk
📞 01366 328258
🕐 Sat-Wed 11.00-17.00

££

I want to go here ☐

GO SEAL WATCHING

...at Blakeney Point

Although you can sometimes spot a seal in a zoo, we think it's far more fun to see them in their natural habitat. So this place definitely wins our *seal* of approval!

Blakeney Point is a strip of sand that stretches out into the sea. It's also a haven for seals – around 500 live in the area, and enjoy sunbathing on the sandbanks.

The Bean family have run boat trips from Morston to Blakeney Point for over 50 years. The boats go right up to the whiskered mammals, who are very friendly (and partial to the odd fish). You can even get out and picnic on the point!

Sticker Scores

5 ROYAL SEAL

4 SIGNATURE SEAL

3 WATERPROOF SEAL

2 WAX SEAL

1 RUBBER SEAL

Photo Op
Become a wildlife photographer and snap a sunbathing seal!

Make A Day Of It

🔑 Giggle at rude art. Cley-next-the-Sea is a pretty village nearby, but the statues in the church are not so polite. Look out for a carving of a man pulling down his trousers, and engravings of mermaids sticking out their tongues.

🔑 See seashells in Glandford Shell Museum. This quirky cottage is filled with unusual shells, fossils and birds.

Top Tip

As well as running ferry trips, the Bean family also sell big bags of mussels. They're great with chips!

Fascinating Facts

★ **There are 33 species of seal worldwide, but only two live in Britain. They are the grey seal and the common seal.**

★ People generally think of seals as swimmers, but they actually spend up to 90 per cent of their lives out of the water sunbathing on the sandbanks. It's just as well they don't suffer from sunburn!

★ **Seals can hold their breath underwater for up to one and a half hours.**

★ Seal is a musician from London who was famous in the 1990s. As far as we're aware he cannot hold his breath underwater for one and a half hours.

PLAN YOUR VISIT 39

Bean's boat trips
69 Morston Rd, Blakeney, NR25 7BD
www.beansboattrips.co.uk

📞 **01263 740505**

🕐 **Three or four departures a day, timetable dependent on tide.**

££

I want to go here ☐

← Sunbathing seals

RIDE A STEAM TRAIN

...on the Poppy Line Railway

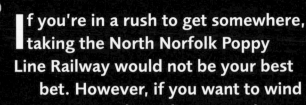

If you're in a rush to get somewhere, taking the North Norfolk Poppy Line Railway would not be your best bet. However, if you want to wind through spectacular scenery, this is the train trip for you!

The Poppy Line links the seaside town of Sheringham to Holt. The steam-train journey between the two is ten miles long and takes you over wooded hills and heaths. Unsuprisingly, the surrounding fields are covered with poppies in summer.

You can hop off at any point (well, any point when the train has stopped!) to look around the stations and marvel at historic trains. The vintage diesel engines are particularly impressive. It's a great way to let off some steam!

Sticker Scores

5	4	3
STEAM TRAIN	HIGH-SPEED SHUTTLE	ELECTRIC TRAM

2	1
RUSTY LOCOMOTIVE	STEAM KETTLE

Similar Spots

The Poppy Line isn't the only old train steaming through Norfolk:

🔑 Bure Valley Railway. This line follows the meandering Bure river through the countryside for eighteen miles. It also passes through Norfolk's longest railway tunnel.

🔑 Wells Harbour Railway. One of four little engines (Edmund, Densil, Howard or Weasil) will run you from Wells Harbour to Wells Beach. There are stops for ice cream along the way.

How do you know when a train is eating toffee?

You hear it *choo*-ing!

← View from the railway

Fascinating Facts

★ The poppy is the county flower of Norfolk. A Victorian writer was so impressed by the fields of flowers that he gave the name Poppyland to the stretch of coast between Cromer and Overstrand.

★ The highest railway station in the world is at Cóndor, in Bolivia. It is at an altitude (height above sea level) of 4,787 metres. That's three and a half times higher than Britain's tallest mountain!

★ The only volcanic railway station was built on top of Mount Vesuvius, in Italy, in 1880. Sadly it was destroyed by an eruption in 1944. Presumably there are now long delays on the line!

PLAN YOUR VISIT 40

North Norfolk Railway

Sheringham Station, Station Approach, Sheringham, NR26 8RA

www.nnrailway.co.uk

📞 01263 820808

🕐 Daily (peak) 09.45-17.40
Daily (out of season) 10.30-15.00
Check website for daily timetables

££

I want to go here ☐

NORFOLK

GO BEACHCOMBING

...at Wells-next-the-Sea

Don't worry, we're not suggesting you take your hairbrush down to the sea! Beachcombing involves searching the beach for interesting items washed up by the waves. So you'll be fine with just a bucket and spade!

The beaches at Wells-next-the-Sea are long, smooth and sandy, which means it is easy to spot unusual objects. Look out for pearly seashells, starfish or maybe even a message in a bottle!

Sticker Scores

5	4	3
PEARLY QUEEN	*MUSSEL MAN*	COAST GUARD

2	1
SEA TRAWLER	BEACH BUM

When you get home, you can use your finds as awesome ornaments or cracking craft projects. Why not make a photo frame far more funky by sticking small shells around the edge?

Make A Day Of It

🔑 Slide down a sand dune. Gun Hill near Burnham Overy Staithe is a huge sand dune that's around sixteen metres high. The views from the top are fantastic, but it's even more fun to slide down to the bottom (on your bottom!).

🔑 Go alpaca trekking. Alpacas are animals that look a bit like small llamas. Pedro, Pablo and their guides will lead you along the coastal path at Wells-next-the-Sea. Bring chopped apples to treat them at the end!

🔑 Bounce to the clouds at Abraham's Bosom. This activity centre near the campsite in Wells-next-the-Sea has trampolines, go-karts and kayaks!

← No comb required!

Fascinating Facts

⭐ **The shells of sea creatures sometimes change colour depending on the food they eat. For example, red seaweed gives some sea animals a reddish shell.**

⭐ If you hold a shell to your ear, you can hear a noise that sounds a lot like the sea. You don't need to be near water for it to work – the *shhhh* noise is caused by sound waves bouncing around inside the shell.

Top Tip

Check the tide times before your visit – a low tide means more beach will be uncovered and ready for combing!

PLAN YOUR VISIT 41

Wells-next-the-Sea
Norfolk, NR23
www.wells-guide.co.uk

FREE

I want to go here ☐

LEARN TO SURF

...at Cromer

- -

When you think of surfing, you probably think of sunny spots with big waves like California or Cornwall. Nonetheless, you'll be pleasantly surprised to know you can ride waves in Norfolk too!

The strip of coast between Cromer and East Runton offers great conditions for beginner surfers.

Glide Surf School is run by experienced instructors who can give individual or group lessons. The school provides a board and a wetsuit to keep you warm (the North Sea can be chilly!).

Glide also offers stand-up paddleboard lessons. Paddleboarding is a bit like surfing, but you stand up and use an oar. You're also less likely to fall off, so we think it's *oar*-some!

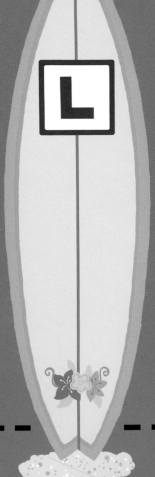

Sticker Scores

5 SURFBOARD

4 WICKED WAVE

3 SWEET SWELL

2 RUBBISH RIPPLE

1 SURF-*BORED*

Best Of The Rest

🔑 Jump in a lifeboat at the RNLI Henry Blogg Museum. This hands-on museum at the end of Cromer pier tells the stories of dramatic sea rescues by local lifeboat crews.

🔑 See a 600,000-year-old elephant at the Cromer Museum. The cliffs at West Runton near Cromer are being rapidly worn away by the weather and power of the tide. This process, called erosion, has revealed the bones of a very ancient trunked creature.

🔑 Walk through a fisherman's house at the Time and Tide Museum in Great Yarmouth.

Fascinating Facts

★ Surfing is thought to have begun on the huge waves of Hawaii. Locals made long boards out of wood . . . though there is no record of whether they wore beads in their hair and called each other dude!

★ Surfers have their own slang language. For example, a *kook* is an inexperienced surfer, *ankle busters* are very small waves and a *ding* is a chip on the surface of the board. (By chip we mean a dent, by the way – a ding is NOT a fried potato served on a surfboard!)

> **What do you say to water when it's covering a beach?**
>
> Hi, tide!

← Surf's up!

PLAN YOUR VISIT 42

Glide Surf School
Brook Street, 1 Clarence Mews, Cromer, NR27 9EY
www.glidesurfschool.co.uk
📞 07966 392227
🕐 Times vary – booking essential
£££

I want to go here ☐

GO ON SAFARI

...at Pensthorpe

You don't have to escape to Africa to go on safari. You can get close to wildlife with binoculars, backpacks and a muddy Land Rover – without leaving Norfolk!

Pensthorpe is a large nature reserve in the Wensum Valley. Its huge wildlife population is continually changing. The wardens keep a diary of all the species they spot – sightings include kingfishers and rare butterflies. Pensthorpe is also home to red squirrels. These endangered nut-nibblers are bred in enclosures in the reserve before being released into the wild.

To explore the hidden corners of Pensthrope book the Wensum Discovery Tour. A camouflaged Land Rover will take you (bumpily) off the beaten track while a warden tells you what to look out for. *Safari* so good!

Sticker Scores

5 — *VAN*-TASTIC

4 — LEGENDARY LAND ROVER

3 — *JEEP* AND CHEERFUL

2 — BORING BUS

1 — BROKEN DOWN

Fascinating Facts

★ Early Land Rovers, made in the 1940s, were all painted a light-green colour. This was because there was a lot of leftover military paint after World War Two.

★ Red squirrels were once the only species of squirrel in the UK, but now they are seriously endangered. That's because in the late 1800s the big bad grey squirrel was introduced from America. Greys pinch the red squirrel's food, and carry a disease which kills reds.

★ Until recently, Thetford Forest (see p84) was home to the last remaining mainland population of red squirrels in southern England. Nowadays reds are only found in Scotland, northern England and on a few isolated islands.

↖ A birds-eye view of Pensthorpe

What do squirrels give each other on Valentine's Day?

Forget-me-nuts!

Top Tip
Pick up a wildlife-tracker trail sheet at the gift shop. Complete it as you explore Pensthorpe and return the sheet to the shop to win a free gift!

PLAN YOUR VISIT 43

Pensthorpe
Fakenham, Norfolk, NR21 0LN
www.pensthorpe.com

📞 01328 851465

🕐 Daily (peak) 10.00-17.00
Daily (out of season) 10.00-16.00

£££

I want to go here ☐

NORFOLK

BAKE YOUR OWN BREAD

...at Bircham Windmill

In the days before supermarkets, people walked from miles around to buy their bread from Bircham Windmill. Based on the sample we tried, we think it's still worth the journey!

Bircham Windmill is one of the few working windmills left in Norfolk. Visitors can climb right to the top and go out on the deck beside the sails. You can see for miles around!

The bakery at the bottom of the windmill uses only flour that is milled on the site. The kids' cookery corner is a chance for you to test out this famous flour – and your own baking skills. The mill owners will provide you with everything you *knead*!

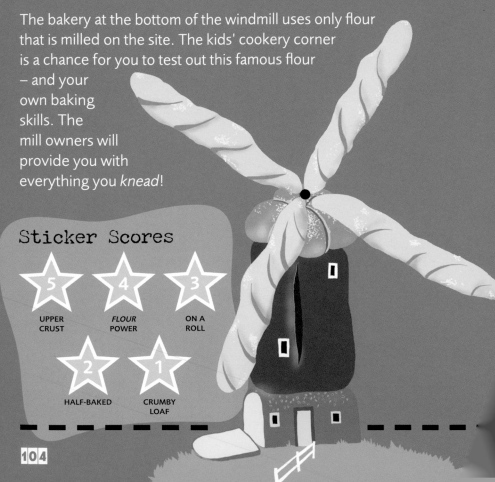

Sticker Scores

5 UPPER CRUST

4 *FLOUR* POWER

3 ON A ROLL

2 HALF-BAKED

1 CRUMBY LOAF

Similar Spots

🔑 Letheringsett Mill is the last remaining water mill in Norfolk that still produces flour. The mill runs daily tours and demonstrations.

🔑 Stow Mill near Mundeseley has been fully restored. It no longer grinds corn, but you can climb to the top and look across to the sea!

🔑 Horsey Mill was a favourite spot for smugglers in the eighteenth century. They used the base to store their loot and send coded messages using the sails when the authorities were approaching.

← Milling about

Fascinating Facts

⭐ **At one point there were more than 100 mills in Norfolk. Most of the smaller ones have now disappeared or fallen into disrepair.**

⭐ Twelve million loaves of bread are made every day in the UK. We eat only eight million of these – the rest goes to waste. *Crumbs!*

⭐ **According to Scandinavian tradition, a boy and girl who eat from the same loaf of bread will fall in love. We're not so sure – we reckon they'll just squabble over who gets the crust!**

Top Tip

Make hedgehog bread! Roll the dough into a ball, make one end pointed like a snout and use a fork to create the prickles. It beats a boring baguette any day!

PLAN YOUR VISIT 44

Bircham Windmill

Great Bircham, King's Lynn, PE31 6SJ

www.birchamwindmill.co.uk

📞 01485 578393

🕐 Daily (peak) 10.00-17.00

I want to go here ☐

WATCH WILD SWANS

...at Welney Wetland Centre

The UK in winter may not seem that tropical to you. But for the arctic birds who fly south at this time of year, Norfolk is practically the Caribbean!

Welney Wetland Centre is a large nature reserve with lots of lagoons (large lakes). It's a superb place to watch up to 9,000 wild swans land after an epic journey.

Each year these amazing travellers fly thousands of miles south from their icy breeding ground in Siberia. They arrive in October and leave in February.

Sticker Scores

5	**4**	**3**
SWAN *LIKE*	GOLDEN GOOSE	SPECIAL CYGNET
2	**1**	
PLUMP PIGEON	UGLY DUCKLING	

The best time to catch the swans is during their dinner. Feeding takes place twice a day, and in the evening the lagoons are floodlit. Fortunately, you can look on from a heated watchtower – not all visitors to Welney enjoy arctic temperatures!

Best Of The Rest

🔑 Go pond-dipping. There are a whole host of creatures to be found under the surface of Welney's water. All equipment is provided.

🔑 Become a bat detective. On certain evenings you can also meet some of Welney's nocturnal visitors. Help the warden locate bats using detectors and infrared cameras.

What happens when you tell a duck a joke?

It *quacks* up!

Fascinating Facts

⭐ **Welney was once a huge centre for outdoor ice skating. The National Speed Skating Championships were held on the lagoons in 1870! Sadly, warmer winters mean that nowadays the wetlands rarely freeze enough to make skating possible.**

⭐ Swans can fly as fast as 60 mph. That's about the same speed as a car driving along a motorway!

⭐ **In Britain all mute swans (the common white birds) in open water officially belong to the Queen. Every July the royal swans on the river Thames are rounded up, marked and then released in a ceremony known as swan upping. We suppose that's *swan* way to keep track of them!**

← Birds on the water at Welney Point

PLAN YOUR VISIT 45

WWT Welney Wetland Centre
Hundred Foot Bank, Welney, Nr Wisbech, PE14 9TN
www.wwt.org.uk

📞 **01353 860711**

🕐 **Daily (peak) 09.00-17.00**
Daily (out of season) 10.00-17.00

£

I want to go here ☐

NORFOLK

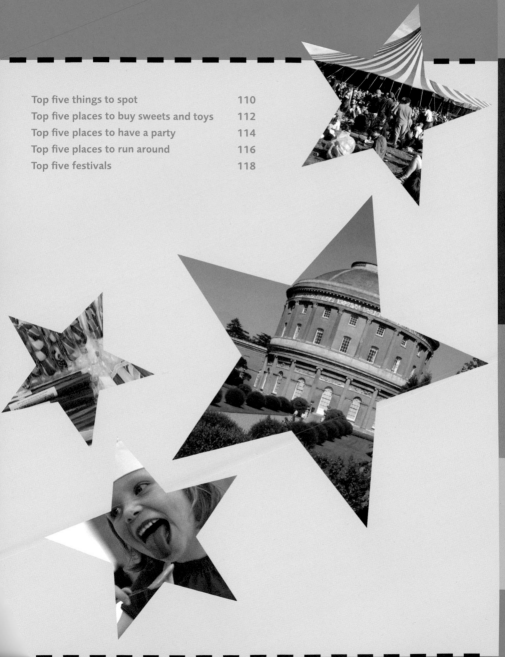

CAMBRIDGE

CAMBRIDGESHIRE

SUFFOLK

NORWICH

NORFOLK

TOP FIVES

TOP FIVE

...things to spot

Whilst you're out and about exploring the region, make sure you keep a look out for these local curiosities!

I SPOTTED:

- [ ] Suffolk Punch
- [ ] Pink Houses
- [ ] Rowers
- [ ] Dragons
- [ ] Gowns

Suffolk Punch

A Suffolk Punch has nothing to do with boxing! It's actually a breed of large horse. The name Punch comes from its solid appearance and strength.

Suffolk Punches are chestnut-coloured and can weigh up to 1,000 kilogrammes – that's the same as a small car! They were traditionally used for farm work. Look out for them in fields and on football shirts (a Suffolk Punch is on the logo of Ipswich Town Football Club).

Pink Houses

Old houses in Suffolk are a jumble of flint, clay, timber and thatch. The region has no quarries or brickworks, so local traditionally made houses from bits and pieces of whatever wa around!

One common feature is pinkish outside walls. In the days before chemical paints, they did this by mixing ox blood or berry juice into the plaster! Look out for the particularly pink village of Long Melford and the colourful cottages of Lavenham.

Rowers   Dragons   Gowns

Head down to the Cam (the river in Cambridge) and you might spot one of the many college rowing teams. If you're lucky, you could even see the famous Cambridge University crew!

You're most likely to see boats on the part of the Cam that runs northeast from Jesus Green. Most contain eight rowers and one cox (the person who steers). Try running alongside a boat and see if you can keep up!

Norwich is full of dragons! Fortunately, few of them breathe fire – most are made from wood or stone . . .

Look for dragon carvings above gateways, on pub signs or as gargoyles on buildings. One of the oldest dragons can be found in the rafters of Dragon Hall – a magnificent medieval merchant's house. Alternatively, visit Norwich on St George's Day and you'll see Snap (the city's dragon) parade through the streets.

When you're walking through Cambridge look out for people wearing long black gowns. This is not a local fashion statement – gowns are the formal dress of Cambridge University.

University formal dress isn't like school uniform because members of the university don't have to wear it every day. Instead, gowns are worn for graduation ceremonies, formal dinners and other special events. Each college varies the design slightly – see if you can spot the difference!

TOP FIVE

...places to buy sweets and toys

Surely nobody needs any persuading that it's handy to know good places to buy toys and sweets! Here are our favourites in the region.

I WENT TO:

- [ ] Fitzbillies Bakery
- [ ] Docwra Rock Factory
- [ ] Build-A-Bear Workshop
- [ ] Auntie Pam's Sweet Shop
- [ ] Cambridge Toy Shop

Fitzbillies Bakery

Docwra Rock Factory

Fitzbillies has fans all over the world. Apparently, some visitors from America liked their cakes so much that they persuaded the bakery to set up an international postal delivery service!

However, you can't beat buying Fitzbillies' cakes from their shop in Cambridge. The Chelsea buns (a sort of big currant cake) are particularly popular – and satisfyingly sticky! Just don't ask how they're made – the owners have kept the recipe secret for 80 years!

Fitzbillies Bakery
52 Trumpington Street, Cambridge, CB2 1RG
www.fitzbillies.co.uk

The Docwra Rock Factory doesn't produce pebbles or lou guitar music. Instead, i makes something much sweeter – sugary sticks of rock with messages running through them!

The Docwra family's factory is the largest rock shop in the world. In the middle of summer, around 80,000 stick leave the store each week. You can go behind the scene to watch the rock being mad And then eat it. *Rock on!*

Docwra Rock Fact
13 Regent Rd, Great Yarm
NR20 2AF

Build-A-Bear Workshop

Auntie Pam's Sweet Shop

Cambridge Toy Shop

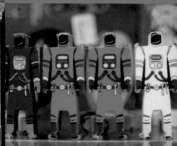

Imagine if you could create a teddy bear exactly how you wanted it. Well, that's the idea behind the Build-A-Bear Workshop!

You first get to choose your favourite furry friend, then you give it a heart, a voice, a name and some clothes. So in other words, the *bear* essentials! You'll even get a birth certificate to take home. We're sure you'll do a *paw*-fect job . . .

Build-A-Bear Workshop

* Chapelfield, Merchants Hall
~per Ground, Norwich, NR2 1SU

w.buildabear.co.uk

Auntie Pam sells good old-fashioned sweets at pocket-money prices. You can buy a single sweet for a penny . . . or buy a whole jar if you prefer!

The selection includes cola cubes, pear drops, toffees and flying saucers. All are lined up temptingly in the window. Many of Auntie Pam's sweets are quite difficult to find in supermarkets or newsagents these days. We think that's a great excuse to stock up!

Auntie Pam's Sweet Shop

3 The Traverse, Bury St Edmunds, IP33 1BJ

01284 765327

This shop is overflowing with toys! There are toys stacked six shelves high and even hanging from the ceiling!

The Cambridge Toy Shop stocks all your favourites, like Lego and Meccano. They also have a great selection of unusual wooden toys that have been handmade by toy experts. Best of all, many of them can be tested out in the shop. It's *toy*-riffic!

Cambridge Toy Shop

29 Hobson Street, Cambridge, CB1 1NL

TOP FIVE

...places to have a party

Many of the places in this book are great for celebrations and events. However, here are a few venues that we think are particularly good for a pleasing party.

I WENT TO:

- [ ] Redwings Horse Sanctuary
- [ ] Hungate Medieval Art
- [ ] Beacon Rally Karts
- [ ] Glazed and Amused
- [ ] Kiddy Cook

Redwings Horse Sanctuary

Having fun is high priority at a party. But if you hold your birthday bash at Redwings you could also help horses at the same time.

Redwings is the largest horse sanctuary in the UK. They care for 1,000 rescued horses, ponies and donkeys, and depend entirely on donations to keep going. A Redwings party includes hands-on grooming sessions, party bags, rosettes and a year's pony adoption for the birthday boy or girl.

Redwings Horse Sanctuary
Hapton, Norwich, NR15 1SP
www.redwings.co.uk

Hungate Medieval Art

At Hungate Medieval Art you can throw a knights and princesses party!

We suggest you ask people to arrive in fancy dress. Tell them to expect a treasure hunt, craft activities and medieval party games. You'll also get a birthday cake like the ones they ate in medieval times. This mysterious old church building is over 600 years old – so it's probably had more birthdays than all your party guests put together!

Hungate Medieval Art
St Peter Hungate Church, Princes Street, Norwich, NR3 1AE
www.hungate.org.uk

Beacon Rally Karts

Glazed and Amused

Kiddy Cook

For an adrenalin-packed party, why not hold your own mini grand prix? Beacon Rally Karts is an exciting off-road karting track that lets you celebrate at high speed.

You won't wear your usual clothes – all party goers get race suits, helmets and gloves. After a short safety lesson, the chequered flag is waved and you can race your friends around the circuit. The birthday boy or girl gets pole position!

Beacon Rally Karts

ealings Rd, Martelsham, oodbridge, IP12 4RP

w.beaconrallykarts.co.uk

If you want really funky plates and bowls at your party, the best thing to do is paint your own.

At a Glazed and Amused party, you and your friends choose a blank plate, bowl, mug or statue to decorate. With some bright paint and big brushes you can create your own crockery masterpiece. Your work of art will then be fired in a kiln for you to collect a week later. It's truly a-*glaz*-ing!

Glazed and Amused

07855 949 811

www.glazedandamused.co.uk

At Kiddy Cook you make your own party meal . . . and you also get to wear a chef's hat!

The Kiddy Cook chefs let you prepare the kinds of food you want to eat. So there's no boiling broccoli or chomping on celery. Instead, you learn how to make sweet treats like ice-cream-cone cakes. Don't worry if you've never cooked before – the chefs are very friendly.

Kiddy Cook

Church Hill, Tasburgh, NR15 1NB

www.kiddycook.co.uk

TOP FIVE

...places to run around

Visiting stuff can be fun, but sometimes you just need to let off steam. So here are five suggestions for great places to run around.

Midsummer Common

This grassy area is great to run around on in the summer. It's also home to some pretty awesome fairs and festivals at other times of year too!

The common hosts an impressive firework display on bonfire night and a marvellous May Day fair. The Midsummer Fair is the most famous and has the biggest rides. Cows also graze on the common – presumably they enjoy the bright lights and *moo*-sic as well!

Midsummer Common
Cambridge, CB4 1HA

Wandlebury Country Park

Wandlebury was once a hill fort, and several ancient skeletons have been unearthed in the park. So keep an eye out for bones as you run around here!

The fort has now vanished, but you can still walk along the Wandlebury Ring – the ditch dug around the edge. It's five metres deep at some points so watch your step. The views from the top of Wandlebury Hill over to Cambridge are, well, *wandle*-ful!

Wandlebury Country
Cambridge, CB22 3AE
www.cambridgeppf.

Plantation Garden

Pigney's Wood Heritage Orchard

Ickworth House Park

In the heart of Norwich there is a secret Victorian garden hidden behind high walls. From the street, you would never guess what lies behind . . .

Those in the know who step inside Plantation Garden will not be disappointed. Set in three acres of land, you'll find fabulous fountains, wonderful woodland walkways and a rocking rockery. If you visit on a Sunday afternoon in summer you'll even find them serving homemade cake!

Plantation Garden
4 Earlham Rd, Norwich, NR2 3DB
www.plantationgarden.co.uk

If you don't know what a Striped Beefing is, Pigney's is the place to find out!

Despite sounding like a multicoloured steak, the Striped Beefing is in fact one of the rare species of apple in this awesome orchard! Pigney's is run by the local community and is dedicated to rescuing rare varieties of Norfolk apples. Take the explorer's trail then pick yourself some apples for free. We reckon you'll live *apply* ever after!

Pigney's Wood
Hall Lane, Napton

Even the most energetic kid wouldn't be able to run around all of Ickworth Park as it covers 1,800 acres!

However, it is a great place to let off some steam – and you can always use their cracking cycling trails if you want to really explore. Look out for all the animals that live in the park. You can marvel at minibeasts, dote on deers, or even badger a badger!

Ickworth House, Park and Garden
Horringer, Bury St Edumnds, IP29 5QE
www.nationaltrust.org.uk

TOP FIVE

...festivals

Everyone likes a good festival, and Cambridge, Norfolk and Suffolk have some of the finest around. Here are five we particularly like.

I WENT TO:

- [ ] World Snail-Racing Championships
- [ ] Latitude Festival
- [ ] Hunstanton Kite Festival
- [ ] Weird and Wonderful Wood
- [ ] Sheringham Carnival

World Snail-Racing Championships

This might not be the fastest race you've ever seen, but it is fiercely contested!

Each July in Congham, hundreds of snails slither 30 centimetres to see if they can win the title of Fastest Snail in the World. Anyone can enter, so why not train your own snail for the event? The winner gets a silver cup stuffed with lettuce. So what are you waiting for? Ready, steady, SLOW!

World Snail-Racing Championships

Congham, Norfolk
www.scase.co.uk/snailracing

Latitude Festival

Latitude is a big three-day festival held in July in Henham Park, near Southwold.

The music is the main attraction, but there's also a cracking kids' arena with drama workshops, puppet shows and story telling. There's a great atmosphere, and some wonderfully weird touches – for example, there are multicoloured sheep roaming around the park! You can either buy a day ticket or camp – either way it's phenomenal festival fun!

Latitude Festival

Henham Park, Southwold, NR34 8
www.latitudefestival.co.u

Hunstanton Kite Festival

Weird and Wonderful Wood

Sheringham Carnival

This high-flying August festival is one of the most colourful events in the region. The organisers don't mind whether the sun shines . . . so long as it's windy!

Throughout the day there are kite-stunt displays by local clubs. Visitors can bring their own kites and receive tips from the experts. There's also a funfair and a classic-car rally to keep you entertained.

Hunstanton Kite Festival

Hunstanton

www.hunstanton-rotary.org.uk

Everyone's heard of rock festivals, but wood festivals are something else altogether!

Each May, over 50 craftspeople gather in Haughley Park to show off their woodwork skills. You can watch displays by makers of musical instruments – including didgeridoos – and wagons. Then, why not take part in one of the workshops on puppet making, jewellery design and den building? You'd be *barking* mad to miss it!

Weird and Wonderful Wood

Haughley Park, Haughley, Stowmarket, IP14 3JY

www.weirdandwonderfulwood.co.uk

This traditional seaside carnival takes place over ten days at the end of July.

The festivities begin with a disco to choose the carnival prince and princess. Then, on the following days, there are awesome events including a sail-hoisting competition, a tug of war and a pantomime-horse race. Our favourite bit is the duck race, which is open to everyone. It *quacks* us up every time!

Sheringham Carnival

Sheringham, Norfolk, NR26

www.sheringhamcarnival.co.uk

PARENTS' PAGE

Greetings, adult. This page is all for you. The rest of the book's for kids, so we thought it was only fair that you had your own page. So if you're a child, stop reading. Now. We said stop. Look, the whole rest of the book's for you. This is just for adults. There's tons more interesting things to do in the rest of the book – why not go to p88 and find out where you can play on the Queen's adventure playground? In fact, we suggest you do anything but read this page. Stop reading right this second. Are you still there? No. Good.

So anyway, hello, adult.

Cambridge, Norfolk & Suffolk Unlocked is for children who are visiting places with adults. Very few of our sites admit unaccompanied children. So as you're likely to be the one planning the trip, we've included site details, such as telephone numbers and opening hours, on each page. Bear in mind that most sites are closed for Christmas, and that last admission is usually earlier than the closing time. We've also specified if there are height or age restrictions. While we have tried hard to ensure all the details are accurate at the time of going to press, things change, so it's best to check before you go anywhere.

Next: the Internet. We've tried to make sure that all our websites are child-friendly, but all the same, we suggest you supervise any surfing. We take no responsibility for third-party content and we recommend you check a site first if you are at all unsure.

Now for some general tips:

- Quite a few venues run good workshops and activities during weekends and school holidays. These are sometimes free, but may require advance booking.
- Many of the activities can be combined into a single day out. Use the maps at the beginning of each section to work out what things are near each other.
- Some of the activities in our book could be dangerous without appropriate adult supervision. Children using this book should be accompanied at all times.
- Many of our free activities in Cambridge, Suffolk and Norfolk involve walks or other locations which don't have opening hours. We recommend you only go during daylight, and make sure you leave enough time to complete the walks.

Oh, and we think it's worth us mentioning that none of the sites in this book pay to be included.

Right then, that's the practical stuff out the way, and there's still a page to fill. So we've selected some facts about Cambridge, Norfolk and Suffolk just for grown- ups. We don't think they're as interesting as the facts in the rest of the book, but then being an adult you don't really like interesting facts, do you now?

- Cambridge, Norfolk and Suffolk are all part of an area that is frequently referred to as East Anglia. Adults sometimes like to debate exactly where the boundaries of East Anglia lie. So we decided not to call this book *East Anglia Unlocked* to prevent people from writing in and complaining that our maps were wrong.

- East Anglia is considered at level two in the Nomenclature of Units for Territorial Statistics. Some grown-ups consider this a useful system for referencing comparable areas in different European countries. But we just think it's NUTS.

- Cambridge is the driest region of Britain and has a more continental climate than the rest of the country. According to the Cambridge University Botanic Garden, the city's 30-year average rainfall from 1970 to 2000 was just 557 millimetres.

- In 1209, a group of scholarly priests and clergymen fled to Cambridge to escape hostile townsmen in Oxford. By 1226, there were enough of them to form their own organisation, and so Cambridge University was born.

- Norfolk is one of the few counties in England that does not have a motorway. The A11 connects Norfolk to Cambridge. (We would list all the other A roads in the county, but we're assuming even adults aren't so boring as to be interested in that sort of thing.)

- The name Norfolk means folk from the North in Anglo-Saxon. Unsurprisingly, the name Suffolk refers to folk from the South. However, the name Norwich does NOT imply it's full of witches from the north.

- Cambridge is renowned for its high-technology centre known as Silicon Fen. This name is a very clever play on words, combining the expression Silicon Valley (a famous technology centre in California) with the word fen, which refers to the flat marshlands surrounding the city.

- C. S. Lewis based the character Puddleglum the Marshwiggle from his book *The Silver Chair* on a stereotypical person from the Fens. Known colloquially as Fenny, Puddleglum is gloomy and miserable most of the time. Thankfully, most people we've met from the Fens are much more cheery.

- Norfolk has 659 medieval churches – the highest concentration in the world. Of these, 120 have round towers, more than any other county in the UK.

- An anagram of EAST ANGLIAN is GENIAL SATAN.

OK, that's your lot. Time to hand the book back to your child. Or, if you are a child who's read all of this, we hope you learned that reading stuff meant for adults just isn't going to be very funny.

INDEX

Here's an index of all the places included in

CAMBRIDGE

CAMBRIDGESHIRE

SUFFOLK

NORWICH

NORFOLK

TOP FIVES

INDEX

Where can you . . .

. . . be active?

. . . find animals?

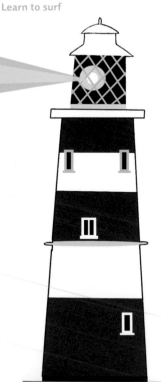

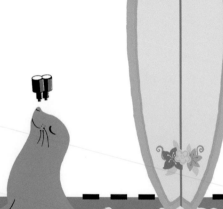

CAMBRIDGE

CAMBRIDGESHIRE

SUFFOLK

NORWICH

NORFOLK

TOP FIVES

...see cool stuff?

...do unusual things?

BACK-OF-THE-BOOK QUIZ

Good Luck!

The answers to all the following questions can be found somewhere in *Cambridge, Norfolk & Suffolk Unlocked*. Email a correct set of answers to us and you'll have a chance to win a signed and framed illustration of your choice from the book!

1 When are swans upped?

2 How long can seals hold their breath under water?

3 What is the county flower of Norfolk?

4 How many horse's legs will be touching the ground in a statue if the rider being represented died in battle?

5 What did students dangle underneath the Bridge of Sighs at St John's College?

6 How many loaves of bread are made every day in the UK?
A. 16
B. 16,000
C. 16,000,000

7 Where is the highest railway station in the world?
A. Eagle in America
B. Cóndor in Bolivia
C. Sparrow in London

8 What is the world record for the number of people inside a bubble?
A. 12
B. 25
C. 33

9 Young knights trained to fight on horseback by riding which animal?
A. Pigs
B. Cows
C. Sheep

10 What is the subject of the world's largest cheese sculpture?
A. The Queen's coronation crown
B. The Duke of Wellington's welly
C. The Prince of Persia's pony

Tie-breaker

In no more than 30 words tell us what is your favourite place in the book and why.

Send your answers to **quiz@factfinderguides.co.uk**

Full terms and conditions are on our website.

Chloe Jeffries

Chloe is a historian who grew up in East Anglia. She still owns a beach hut there. She has lots of recipes featuring Ely eels, but not many friends who are bold enough to try them. Chloe loves nothing better than a blustery walk along the Suffolk coast.

Joshua Perry and Emily Kerr

Josh and Emily were at school together, which they think is a great start for setting up a children's publishing company. They spent several years studying in the region, and are rather fond of it. Emily loves the Sedgwick Museum of Earth Sciences, where she's been many times to look at its dinosaur skeletons. Josh is a fan of Pensthorpe, because they have red squirrels there.

Allison Curtis

Allison loves dogs and also used to own two ducks, called Francis and Firkin. She was once part of a successful world record to have the most people bouncing on space hoppers at the same time. She is very keen to visit the seals at Blakeney Point.

Vicky Scott

Vicky decided she was going to be an illustrator when she was five years old. People say she looks a bit like a cartoon character; she quite likes this. She particularly enjoyed drawing Queen Elizabeth slurping tea, and the windmill made of bread.

CREDITS

Author: Chloe Jeffries
Series Editors: Joshua Perry, Emily Kerr
Design: Allison Curtis

Illustrations: Vicky Scott
Maps: Allison Curtis, with reference to
OpenStreetMap – a free, editable map of the world

Thank you to ...

Chloe

Mum, Dad and Dan for dragging me to many of the sites first time around. Mum, Dad and Dan for agreeing to be dragged to many of the sites this time around. Etheldreda, for founding a small but perfectly formed city. Bicycles, for allowing a non-driver to explore. Johnny for getting me the gig. D.Phil for giving me the flexibility to accept. Gav, for proving that the pun is mightier than the sword. Mini Milk sticks for other jokes. All those who work at the featured sites for their help, suggestions and many megabite attachments. Emily and Josh for boundless enthusiasm. Vicky for that stunning Queen Liz.

Emily, Josh, Vicky, Allison

Everyone who has bought and said nice things about our first four books. Nicole Holmes for being an excellent intern. All the sites and bookshops who have supported us as a small publisher. Nicola, Weezy and Luc for putting up with the mobile office in the front room. Italians for making our coffee machine. Jan Belza for a wonderful weekend in Cambridge. Skype for being one of the best business tools in the world. Family Perry and Family Kerr for ongoing support and help with our launches. Flickr photographers for their photos. The internet for introducing Vicky to the *Unlocked* team. Undiscovered second cousins (that would be Vicky again). Everyone else (you know who you are).

Photo Credits